Journeys
in
Dream
and
Imagination

Journeys

in

Dream

and

Imagination

Artur Lundkvist

Introduction by Carlos Fuentes

Translated from the Swedish by
Ann B. Weissmann and Annika Planck

Four Walls Eight Windows

New York

A Four Walls Eight Windows First Edition

First Printing October 1991
Second and Third Printings March 1992

This English-language edition includes selections from the Swedish original.

Printed in the U.S.A.
Cataloging-in-Publication Data:
Lundkvist, Artur, 1906–
[Färdes 1 drömmen och föreställningen. English]
Journeys in dream and imagination / Artur Lundkvist; introduction by
Carlos Fuentes ; translated from Swedish by Ann B. Weissmann and
Annika Planck. — 1st ed.
p.   cm.
Translation of : Färdes 1 drömmen och föreställningen.
ISBN 0-941423-67-0/$17.95
I. Title
PT9875.L74F3413   1991
839.7'172—dc20

Four Walls Eight Windows
Post Office Box 548
Village Station
New York, New York 10014

Design: Martin Moskof
Published in association with Palisades-Amsterdam Communications, Inc.

Table of Contents

FOREWORD

In *October, 1981, the eminent* poet Artur Lundkvist suffered a near-fatal heart attack. It occurred while he was giving a speech on the English writer Anthony Burgess. Abruptly, Lundkvist simply slumped over and then fell to the ground comatose.

In such cases, everything happens very quickly. The blood pressure falls drastically. The flow of oxygenated blood to the brain ceases. In a couple of seconds, there is no more muscle tone. There is sudden unconsciousness.

Two years later, Artur Lundkvist would remember how he began his lecture. After that, nothing. This is typical. The disturbed functions of the brain, which lead to unconsciousness, also lead to total loss of memory. The function of memory needs several seconds to become operative in the brain. When the metabolism of the brain suddenly ceases to function, the last bits of memory are not readied for further use. Such semifinished memory products are simply not saved.

For the next two months, Artur Lundkvist, at the age of 75, lay in a coma in the intensive care unit of the hospital. That he survived at all bears witness to the strength of these departments today. Particularly in the case of heart or lung problems, long stays in intensive care units are fraught with danger. These include grave risks from infections. At the same time the balance of fluids in the body must be meticulously monitored, bedsores must be avoided, and proper nutrition must be restored.

After two months, miraculously, Artur Lundkvist woke up. His memories from this time are fragmentary. He recalls bits and pieces: the interior of his hospital room, the view of the railroad station outside. But the memories are disconnected and out of sequence. Events appear as bits and pieces of a puzzle that don't fit together. There is a feeling of everything being slightly bizarre. The situation is complicated by the fact of Artur's tracheotomy, a breathing tube inserted into his throat. The first sign of awareness, of being awake, was a sudden smile, says Lundkvist's wife, Maria Wine. The occasion was the telling of a funny story by a good friend, who had spent a great deal of time by the poet's bedside. The smile spread over Artur's entire face. The following day, the breathing tube was removed, and the next day Maria heard Artur's voice. "Maria," he said, "you are going through so much trouble on my account." As both Maria and Artur tell it, the moments of wakefulness, and clarity, grew longer and longer. It was just before Christmas, 1981.

At the same time, Artur Lundkvist began dreaming, richly and strangely. "I traveled further than I ever have before," he said. Many of the trips were filled with great joy. They included visits to many countries on various continents all across the globe. He traveled by air over Vietnam, and to a foreign planet where Swedish immigrants had brought their cows, which now gave blue milk. He met and spoke with persons long dead, and visited a railroad station in Chicago, where doctors operated on white people and made them black.

Strange dreams of the kind described here, with strongly meaningful content, are often reported by patients who have been on the heart-lung machine, as Artur Lundkvist was while in a coma. He asked me why, behind his "open eyes," he continued to have such strange dreams. I could not give him an answer to this. We do not know why our brains begin to manufacture images and impressions of sights and sounds—even music—after we have experienced lack of oxygen or altered ventilation in our bodies. What we do know is that the resurrection of the brain's functions takes a great deal of time. The membranes of the nerve cells must be restored, the signaling systems (the synapses) must be reconstructed, leaking capillaries have to be fixed, broken molecules need to be cleansed away.

All this takes a good deal of time, during which the nerve cells do not function as links to other parts of the brain. Groups of brain cells become over-active. Sometimes, although not in Artur Lundkvist's case, cramps occur. After an acute attack of deoxygenation, the patient is often in a state of semi-awareness or half-sleep, when impressions of reality and the functions of the brain are intermingled. There is very little control over what happens to the psyche. The same phenomenon, although to a much lesser degree, occurs during normal sleep.

I asked Artur about his capacity to read and write, to understand new ideas or create them. The thought of living without creating, without writing, struck him as horrible. Artur Lundkvist is not a sentimental person. Certainly, it was difficult for him to awake to doubt and despair. In February, 1982, he attempted for the first time to read a novel in Spanish. It was a slow process, but he was able to do it. His knowledge of five foreign languages was still intact, as was his joy of reading and comprehending. The first nightmarish vision of opening a book and finding all the pages blank was gone. During the first long year of convalescence, many were there to help. But it was Maria who sat by his side every day and read page after page to him, sang to him, and read poetry. He would remember hardly any of this.

During the subsequent years of his convalescence, Artur Lundkvist became productive again, writing and editing many articles and books. He mentioned to me that prior to his illness he never feared death, experiencing only the slight irritation, or frustration, of not knowing what death was really all about. I asked him if coming out of the coma state, awakening, was difficult. He said it was. He described the first insights as terribly difficult and painful—a form of cosmic weariness combined with more immediate worries about the future. He was troubled when he pondered the possibility of the loss of his ability to write in the Swedish language.

Our conversation lasted more than two hours, and Artur was tired at the end of it. He said he tires more easily now than before. Returning to the subject of death, he added: "But I know what happens now. It finishes. The world disappears. It is quite simple."

—David Ingvar, M.D.,
Professor and Chief of the
Department of Clinical
Neurophysiology Medical
Clinic, The University of
Lund, Sweden

Adapted from an article by Dr. Ingvar which appeared in the Swedish newspaper *Svenska Dagbladet*.

PREFACE

(Here my wife Maria tells the story of my illness from her side, and of the awakening from coma of which I myself have no memory. A.L.)

S*uddenly, you were gone, and yet* not quite gone:

you lay there with large, open, astonished eyes, as if something invisible had interrupted their last visual impression, your pupils were wordless like black, lackluster stones, yet in the greyish-blue iris of your eyes there was a hint of a milky white shimmer,

you were on the respirator, seeing nothing, hearing nothing, unable to move, not reacting when spoken to, when I held your hand there was no response but your hand was neither cold nor warm,

yes, all that which is you, your lively gestures, your broad smile, your joy in fighting and story-telling had been taken away from you: your rest from yourself was threateningly close to the longest rest of all,

your face was dreamlike and still, you were like a "dreamer with open eyes," but within your body there raged a battle of life and death, one moment you were breathing heavily, the next minute you almost stopped breathing, only gasping for air with a ferocity that scared me,

did you feel pain or didn't you ... how would I know... the EKG curves rose and fell, sharp mountain tops or creeping low hills, your pulse was either too slow or much too fast,

anxiously, I watched this battle, of which you yourself were unaware, fearful that the pulse and the rise and fall of the EKG curves would stop without warning, we who had suddenly been called to your sickbed felt immobilized, there was an almost sacred silence around you,

it was difficult to leave you, leave you there alone without being able to help, but what could I do but go home . . .

oh, the emptiness and the silence that met me when I entered the apartment, not to be met by you at the door or not to hear the noise from your rattling typewriter, and then not knowing how long this emptiness would last, yes, it was as if all things in the apartment had already begun turning away from me and a feeling of unreality was creeping upon me—until the telephone started ringing and ringing: the reporters were unmercifully pushy, I was startled every time the phone rang, afraid to answer and afraid not to answer.

For two months, you were unconscious but during that whole long time I never spoke the word of which I feared the meaning,

every morning around six, I called the hospital and always got the same answer: your condition was unchanged, somehow that comforted me, a very, very small hope grew inside me,

twice a day I came to you, I sang to you, I read poems, I played music by some of your favorite composers, I spoke to you of shared experiences, I called your name into your ear, begged you to come back to me, I searched your eyes for the slightest sign of life, I cried at your bedside but never aloud, I didn't want you to hear it,

I was there when they gave you nourishment intravenously, when the nurse gave you injections, spoke to you reassuringly, I looked at her when she dropped the fluid of life into your eyes, staring wide open but still not seeing, as soon as I left your room, I longed to come back again in the evening and I always stayed until the night nurse arrived, it reassured me to see and speak to the one who would watch over you, and before I fell asleep, I felt comfort knowing it would soon be morning and then I could return to you.

The doctors had no encouraging words for me, you entered into a difficult crisis, your heart became weaker, and your breathing was once more so painful to listen to, it was easy to believe you would not make it,

I continued to visit you every morning and every night, refusing to accept the thought—and much to the surprise of us all, you survived the crisis, and your breathing returned to near normal,

after you had been in a coma for a month and a half, it seemed to me that you began to react when I read to you and that when I stopped reading, there was a listening expression in your eyes as if you wanted to hear more, often I read one of my own poems, "Awake, lake of the forest," one that I knew to be among your favorites,

when I told the doctors what I had discovered they didn't believe me, but I insisted, and finally they asked me to let them be there when I read to you, and I believe they were convinced: it was not merely my wishful thinking leading me astray, you were actually on your way out of the coma.

The first sign of your awakening occurred soon after, and strangely enough, it was the same good friend who had been there to give you mouth-to-mouth resuscitation when you fell who again managed to bring a smile to your lips,

one evening, he spontaneously took your hand in his and said: "Artur, I am going to tell you a funny story!" and you appeared to be listening to it, because shortly thereafter, a smile lit up your face, it soon disappeared again, but encouraged by this smile, your friend told you another story and your smile returned, I hardly dared believe you were returning from your coma but your smile stayed with me as if to comfort me when I fell asleep,

a few days later, the breathing tube was removed and you were able to speak immediately, your moments of being unconscious grew shorter and shorter, I could have longer conversations with you, and on Christmas Day, the director of the hospital called to congratulate me: he and your attending physicians were now convinced that you would recuperate, I cried tears of joy and exhaustion.

—Maria Wine

INTRODUCTION

S*ome books are forever sealed* within their first utterances: *It was the best of times, it was the worst of times . . .*; *Longtemps, je me suis couché de bonne heure . . .*; *En un lugar de la Mancha, de cuyo nombre non quiero acordarme . . .*; *Call me Ishmael.*

Beauty and paradox are reconciled in these first words. Dickens' sweeping rhetorical opening leads in the end to Sydney Carton's moving surrender at his own death (*It is a far, far better thing that I do . . .*); Proust's narrator will hardly ever sleep again, endlessly remembering; Don Quixote, by forgetting willfully and willfully shedding doubt on his place of origin, his authorship, his genre and his name, creates the principle of uncertainty on which the modern novel is founded; and Melville's Ishmael must be others if he is to be himself.

I know I am traveling all the time. So begins Artur Lundkvist's chronicle of two months of immobility, of unconsciousness, of technical death. It is a stunning paradox. Reading, we soon realize that it is a desperate paradox as well. The author is "imprisoned in a completely flat world where I can only rest on my back and breathe." What solace then can he find in reminding himself, as he does, that where he lies the "rotational speed of earth is approximately 240 meters a second . . . a speed far exceeding that of any gale?" Solace, or the risk of the even greater death of the spirit and the will?

A Rilkean sense of danger is present, more urgent than the seemingly imminent event of death. If the air were not there to protect us (even as we lay dying), the earth's own movement would level the world to "one single, terribly agitated ocean." An eerie sense of equilibrium permeates Lundkvist's book from the beginning. As he rests in bed, unconscious, the earth is traveling around the sun, at some thirty kilometers a second, and talking to him.

Displacement is the action of literature, whether this means leaving one's village to discover the world, abandoning the world of gods and their myths to create the myths of man, or finding one's way back home; whether it means leaving one's own skin to become another, journeying, like Xavier de Maistre, around one's room or, like Jules Verne, to the center of the earth. Literature is finally the vessel by which, as Freud points out, the labor of life is transfigured by the work of dreams. In displacement, substitutions between what we were, what we are, and what we hope to be, take place—or rather, take leave.

In Lundkvist's journeys in dream and imagination, a radical immobility is surrounded by an endless movement. Call the movement dream, metamorphosis, nature, word, voice, desire. It is all of these. From the center of the paradox, once established, all things may flow, but none can ever return. The paradox of Artur Lundkvist, immobile traveler, sunk in the realms of the unconscious, dreaming the sleep of silence, working in the dream of death, is that only something outside the paradox can give it life.

Transformation, free or determined, is the immediate response of the immobile traveler to the paradox. Everything, we are reminded, can become rigid. And the reverse is also true. The extreme immobility of what is frozen beckons the utmost mobility of fluid metamorphosis. The ice melts. A river can rise above the surrounding land until it flows into the sky.

In our imagination, we change what we cannot control: Look, there is a volcano spewing milk instead of fire. We also assign to nature our own human lassitude as we lie unconscious on a hospital bed: no echo "can stand its task forever"; the river Tigris grows weary of washing "the soiled linen of others"; even man-made objects suffer a kind of decline towards death: "... there are statues that have been standing so long that their legs have varicose veins."

There is a danger lurking here in the dreams of the immobile traveler: that metamorphosis can be little more than a mirror where change occurs, as in a Marx Brothers routine, in near-perfect, willful, and ludicrous mimicry. There is no glass in the mirror, just ourselves and nature, face to face. As nature changes, so do we; as we change, so does nature. This symmetrical mimesis can lead to sheer immobility, "rain like a river that stopped flowing," so that the search for a way towards renewed motion is foiled.

Metamorphosis, by definition, is not self-contained. And we cannot dominate nature by resembling her. The immobile traveler at first desires this identification, believes that he has overcome his paradox and settles into the comforting world of simile, where things resemble one another. But since he is a poet, he is soon dissatisfied. He wants something more, he wants to unite the two terms of the comparison in a metaphor. And so it is Lundkvist the poet who tempts the paradox, is the sorcerer of the metamorphosis, and refuses to fall into the trap of easy identifications: You think you are a seal? You wish you were a swan? You want to believe that rivers grow weary of washing? Well, think, desire, and believe some more; you are barely scratching the surface of the terrible truth, the scars of your unsheltered, radical loneliness. You are part of nature, which has nurtured you and given you your being, but you will cease to be if you do not separate yourself from the embrace of nature.

There is no equilibrium between man and nature. There is conflict; there is tragedy; we are both right. We must exploit nature in order to survive. But nature will always survive us (unless nuclear holocaust determines that we both die simultaneously). Metamorphosis can be the end of our nostalgic desire to recover the unity and happiness that never were. We are born and we shall die of conflict and separation, "damaged," as Adorno says. The problem is to transform differences (since we cannot fully recreate unity) into values.

"You have feet but not roots, that is the difference between the trees and you." But the bear moves, and the seal, and the horse, and the river. So it is not movement alone that sunders you from nature, but the quality of the motion or the stillness. You can only feign that you love the ocean by caressing it; the ocean would demand as an act of love that you drown in it. The sun suffers unendingly and owes us nothing. Over nature, even its most microscopic forms, hovers a totality, infinite, indifferent to us. We are never that totality, but only one of the minor forms of nature (you lie flat on your bed and stare at the ceiling): We can never truly merge with fire, water, earth or air; the human form is always alien to the elements.

The dilemma of being devoured by nature or expelled from nature can only be solved through art. History is what separates us; art is what unites us; we cannot shun either term; neither can we fully conciliate them, between themselves or in their relation to nature. Poetry is our attempt to bind anew, at their most basic, human level, the natural and the historical. The writer's task is to recover the original document, Croce once said of *The Iliad*, where history and poetry are identical. That is, perhaps, the unending work of the man traveling flat on his back during a two-month simulacrum of death. Call him Artur Lundkvist.

But do not call it death. To be dead, writes Milan Kundera, is to lose the past, not the future. Lundkvist goes one step further: once death arrives, he writes, it is as if we had never existed. "There is no meaning to our having lived," for death never attempts, by itself, anything beyond itself.

Yet in the well of unconsciousness, in the imitation of death, the poet finds a desire to return to "our old world . . . with its unending waiting, the unbearable pain of its memories."

Lundkvist proposes an image of death which we also find in Aztec mythology: A "shadow dog" approaches to lead us into Hell. But Lundkvist's dog becomes uncertain of its mission, hesitates, "lies down or turns around, starts walking away, but remains silent." As silent, indeed, as the unconscious poet, whose muteness is "like a fine spiderweb against my face." He cannot rub it off, he adds. But he can name the silence. Even in this absence which is his own, even in this apartness resembling death, he can *name* all of this. He is not dead because he can *sustain* names even if he cannot say them. He can know silence. The seal, the swan, the trees, the sea and the powerful horse do not know the name of silence.

Call it not metamorphosis, or nature, or death; call it words, call it voice. Call it the fall of the universe of things if words are not there to name them.

A tender Volpone, Artur Lundkvist is in the world but the world has given up on him; he is there, but silent, he is not there. He loses his handwriting ability. It is determined that he will probably be condemned to a wheelchair existence for the rest of his days. He can't

19

hold his spoon straight. He brings his food to his ear. It is predicted that he "will never again function with a semblance of normality."

Yet he will fool them all, because he has never been beaten, he has simply been, all this time, at the center of an unfathomable mystery without being conscious of it; but in this does he not resemble each and every one of us? In this, has he not revealed, through his experience of death, dream and imagination, that his is not a unique experience but rather a new arrival, beyond the simile of man and nature, beyond the paradox of the immobile traveler, at the epiphany where our awareness of humanity is our innermost self? Others have been there before, Dante and Goethe, Thomas Mann (not Cervantes, not Shakespeare, not the rousing, all-embracing starters, but the great, serene, crepuscular enders). It is the epiphany of the European consciousness, fearfully demonstrative: Your awareness of humanity is your innermost you.

Lundkvist's *Journeys in Dream and Imagination* is the most moving milestone of Europe's renewal. It is a return from the edge of darkness; the regaining of consciousness; a word, a voice, a name we share and love.

—Carlos Fuentes

Journeys
in
Dream
and
Imagination

I *know I am traveling all the* time, possibly with no interruptions, also with no tremors or noises, soundlessly and softly, and then I am no longer lying in my bed but stepping out into the world where everything is awake, sundrenched, comforting, and I am there clearly as a visitor, and I am quite at ease,

it must be a dream journey I have undertaken, a definite dream journey where all is real but where all my wishes are fulfilled without my even asking, precisely the way all journeys ought to be, but maybe one has to be dead in order to journey like that,

by the way, how can I know I am not dead, even though I have no sensation of being dead, and it is as if I rest in a middle zone without feeling either warmth or cold or hunger or any human needs

N*o wind, not even the slightest* breeze, complete stillness and silence, yet I am traveling or have a definite sense of traveling, but how can it happen without a sound or feeling of movement,

can I travel motionless or glide onwards without the least resistance from the earth or the air, can it be that time has stopped or speed no longer has a meaning, that I have reached the crossroads beyond motion and stillness . . .

but yet I am here, can feel my body and sense my breathing, it is a nothingness that is definite, but without any wind or air or sound whatsoever, as if all but my own being has ceased existing,

it amazes me somewhat, but it actually does not matter, why should I need wind and sound, that which exists does exist nevertheless, and I must be the one perceiving it, and that is surely sufficient to make me alive and capable of perceiving,

I do not know what time has passed, but now I begin hearing something, at first vaguely, then with increasing strength, and soon, I can recognize a distant song by women, a choir like in a church but heard from a distance, the song rises and falls rhythmically, with different voices blending, lighter ones and darker ones,

it is actually not beautiful, but it still makes an impression by its inherent certainty and power, yes, the song bears witness of a conviction that conquers silence and nothingness, as if journeying by its own force and conquering all resistance,

I feel that I am again traveling, that immobility and silence no longer reign, but I do not know what the women are singing or what the song means, it is simply there, filling the room which was only silence and emptiness

I *must be on a ship, out at sea,* a multitude of birds are flying very close, I can clearly see the markings on their wings and the color of their eyes like pearls of white, brown, red, and black, they are flying quietly close to one another, staying together like a flock of migrant birds, it is as if they were all tied together by an invisible cord

A*gain, birds are flying by, they* come in close waves with short breaks between them, some are striped like zebras in black and white, not particularly beautiful, but easily distinguished at a distance, like the black and white bars that block a road,

some have spots of red, like bushes covered with roses, unnecessarily decorated for merely flying over the empty sea, some are entirely white with yellow spots on their breasts, as if a sun were glowing inside them, yet other birds are painted in a cubist fashion, with sharp angles and curves, brilliantly colored with red against blue and yellow against green, as if they were camouflaged for living in the jungle,

birds you would hardly ever see otherwise but who evidently exist in various parts of the world, where the eyes of man rarely reach

The silence is like a fine spiderweb against my face, I cannot rub it off, it is simply there without being tangibly real, it does not flutter like a leaf in the breeze, nor is it entirely immobile, it feels like the impression of a wind that is already becalmed, it is hardly the beginning of the weave and it does not betray a pattern, it is the most insignificant matter, yet it makes itself known ℘

I*t is a river with very thin water* and the bottom is even like a paved road, almost like a highway, but it is still a river and the horses pulling me are trotting along with a light clattering of hooves and the carriage rolls through the thin water with a faint whistle, without swaying at all, as if it were rolling along on soundless rubber wheels, nor does it rock at all, but the pavement seems absolutely smooth,

it is a comfortable way to travel, far superior to cars and trains, one is closer to the scenery and nothing disturbs the peace of nature, the stillness and silence of the landscape, all is immobile like in a painting, except that it passes by at an even pace,

birds are not frightened by our passage, as if they would neither see nor hear us, they fly so close that one can feel the wing beats close by,

the surroundings barely change, there are fields and meadows but no houses, a clean and well-tended landscape but apparently without inhabitants, nor are there any cattle or other animals,

evening and nightfall come without a sunset, nor does darkness fall, but an opal-colored light shines everywhere, no stars can be seen, nothing but a pale sky,

it seems improbable that we would soon reach an inhabited place, this quiet empty landscape without people seems endless, but this makes me neither impatient nor anxious,

I accept it without question, to be without distance in time and space, merely being something that exists in its own right, without a destination to reach, without unimportant problems and circumstances, without any human needs to attend to

T*hey come at night, they come* even if I don't call for them, nor want anything from them, they almost always come in pairs, these women of the night are much bigger than those of the daytime, softer, more motherly, they know what to do without my saying anything if I have made a mess of my bedlinens without noticing, or wet them without yet feeling the wetness turn to cold,

they make my bed while I lie with open eyes, following their movements, big and sweeping, neat, and they smile a little, their large faces seem to me to be Asiatic, broad, and dark,

they leave quietly, turn off the lights, close the door to the room, I am left alone with the impression of their presence remaining with me, an impression of their dark and powerful appearance, of the silence and emptiness they have left behind, it is like a visit of supernatural beings who have left me there with only sleep to accompany me, like a vague, motherly veil, where I glide into the more clear and present state of dreams,

these women of the night come by one or by two like sisters, they are seldom the same, some have fine hair like halos around their faces as around street lamps in the fog, they are soft and generous, they never chastise me, they do not speak Finnish but they are easy to understand, and yet they speak with a definite Finnish accent, lilting and rhythmical, closer to both lakes and forest than we are, it seems to me that they leave a scent of honey behind, the scent comes from their hair and I imagine that they carry bees in their hair,

they are still strangely real ❡

I*t is the dog returning, the same* dog or a different one, a shadow dog I cannot clearly perceive, it has no definite form or color, it approaches me somewhat threateningly, with a purpose, but then it becomes uncertain, hesitates, lies down or turns around, starts walking away, but remains silent,

maybe it is quite harmless, just seems to want something without knowing what, maybe it is looking for company or a stroking hand, someone who will talk to it, someone who will treat it as a human being,

it might be an unfortunate soul imprisoned in its fur, in its dog-like apparition, it keeps approaching me, maybe hoping each time that I am the human it is looking for, the one who will recognize it and give it a right to exist,

the dog remains totally silent, does not yelp or whine, maybe so as not to disturb me or even frighten me, or maybe it has no voice,

should I do something for this dog, attempt to call it close to me, reach out to stroke its fur... but I am not particularly fond of dogs and I do not quite trust this dog in spite of the compassion that eventually fills me,

I try to talk to it when it approaches me again, but no, it is more apprehensive than before, it is as if it wants me there, but immobile and silent, sometimes it disappears after a while as if prematurely giving up even trying to come close, it may not show up for two or three days, and then it returns as if nothing has happened,

this dog confuses me more and more, we have nothing in common and yet, there seems to already be some kind of connection between us, as if, against my wishes, I have become its lord and master, responsible for its destiny, as if it were a part of my own destiny

I *wake up and find myself in sur-*
roundings with no vertical dimension, the room seems to
close just above me, leaving me no space at all to sit up, I am
forced to lie there straight on my back, unable to turn on my
side,

even if I manage to move
around a little, it does not change my situation, my freedom
of mobility is just as limited however I try to move forwards
or backwards, it is as if I were imprisoned in a completely
flat world where I can only rest on my back and breathe, at
least there is still enough air and I don't have to suffocate,
there is semidarkness around me, and I perceive the room on
both sides and in front of me,

more and more, a suffocating
anxiety gets hold of me, a terrible sense of claustrophobia, I
feel my heart beating violently, I make an effort to keep calm
and find some comfort, maybe something will happen to
change my situation, and I decide to stay where I am, flat on
my back, without moving noticeably, after all, I have no
other choice,

I can lie there and breathe nor-
mally, the best thing would be if I could go to sleep, during
sleep I might be able to tolerate this feeling of being closed
in, and perhaps I would wake up to a normal, four-dimen-
sional world,

now the horrifying thought
comes to me that maybe I am in a coffin without having the
slightest idea how I ended up there, possibly already considered dead,

I am beginning to imagine a
very low but vast basement, I see no way of getting out of
this space, I had better stay where I am, waiting for what
might happen 🐉

Maria, *you are there and you* are not there, I cannot see you but maybe hear you, you are reading poems aloud, and I sense them as if without words, as if they penetrated into me without the aid of words,

I experience time as neither light nor dark, it is neither day nor night, and the hours do not go by, yet time is moving somehow, there are no days, no nights, it is just a journey through time or space, I do not know if I am lying in the same place or if I am traveling without interruption,

sometimes I seem to wake up for a moment, I can see the room I am in, shapes, I can vaguely see some people, faces approaching me and leaning over me, taking form, becoming enlarged, mouths speaking without my being able to hear what they are saying, if I try to say something I immediately sink back into my dreamlike state

W*ith my hands I caress your* knees and imagine they are birds' nests, and now, suddenly, birds fly out from your knees and flutter about the room, not big and clumsy birds like sparrows but small siskins and chickadees with fine and clear chirps, as if they were the violin strings of the symphony of birds,

the little birds fly around the room, seemingly with no feeling of being cooped up, as if they had enough space,

by and by they return to your knees, to their nests, and disappear in their birds' nests I caress again, the birds all quiet and still in there, in their soft nests 🐦

*S*ometimes *I hear someone sing, but* I cannot hear who it is, maybe it is not a single voice but many, sometimes I clearly discern that it is Maria singing, and she is singing a Danish folk song which I particularly like, it is such a sad and disappointed tune, about love never allowed to develop and be fulfilled, and it starts like this:

> 'Twas Saturday by evening
> I sat awaiting you
> you promised you would be there
> but never came to me.
>
> I laid me on my bedstead
> and cried so bitterly
> each time the door was opened
> I thought it might be you—

I can listen to this song until tears fill my eyes, I feel at once as the one betrayed and as the betrayer, it is Maria's voice I hear but she is not there, I am alone in the room, and in my memory only I hear her sing:

> But where can one find roses
> if roses there are none,
> say where can love be truly found
> if love is long since gone

Two women walk into my room and come close to my bed, or maybe they are already standing on either side of the bed, two statuesque and motherly women in white who ask me how I am feeling, if I have been able to sleep and if I feel comfortable, one of them takes my hand and feels my pulse, as if a thread of my life flows into her and meets her in a greeting,

then they disappear and I sink back into my lonely bed, but no longer fully alone, still somehow surrounded by the presence of the two women, they have opened up the blinds halfway, and the early morning light creeps in to keep me company,

in a little while, someone will come with my breakfast tray and serve me in bed, feed me like a small child, and all the while I am lying there staring out through the window, it is a late winter morning with clear, sharp sunshine and a view of a railroad yard, trains with rail cars standing still, waiting to begin their journey, there is snow between the rails, and an engine drives up to them and stops, the wooden houses begin to look chilled, some school children emerge from the houses and move along the street, dressed for winter, beyond the tracks there is a street with very little traffic, mostly cars, everything quiet as if my entire view were wrapped in white cotton

How *difficult it is to come back* to life, how easy to travel through dreams and experience anew that which you have already been through, or things that have never been experienced,

now, you must not only try to remember your own name but also your age, what year it is, where you are, where you live, and all other things self-evident to normal memory,

when I look out the window I do not recognize the city outside, I can't really believe that it is any part of Stockholm, rather, I have a feeling that I am in Malmo, and I don't know why, I look out over a railroad yard where I see trains come and go, and a street with shops and hotels, totally unknown to me, in the background a church spire which I have never seen before, and up close houses and a street with children going off to school and with a rooftop, someone is working on it, there are planes flying by, and reality seems full of activity although it appears to be a cold and clear winter morning,

I am the only one lying in a bed and a nurse's aide looks in on me now and then, sometimes someone brings me food and I try to eat what is put in front of me, but I can't hold the spoon straight and spill the contents when I try to bring the food to my mouth but instead lift it to my ear,

when someone brings me a newspaper I can barely read the large print, I have difficulty bringing the letters together, making words out of them, and even more difficulty finding a meaning in them,

when I have visitors I recognize the faces but cannot remember their names and when I am told, I immediately forget them and someone has to repeat them to me ☙

Maria *is almost always there in* the room but I can't always remember her name, however, I never ask for it, I particularly like it when she reads to me or sings something, the simplest folk songs or rhymes can move me so that tears run down my cheeks, but it is difficult to understand the context and meaning of what she is reading, it is much easier when she tells me a story, and she often does that,

I have a feeling that she is spending too much time caring for me and not leaving enough time for herself, I have guilt feelings for taking so much of her time but she tells me not to worry, I must simply regain my strength and lie there without worrying about anything,

but the doctors apparently do not think highly of my recuperation, it almost seems to me that they see it as an insult to them personally and to their gloomy prognoses, even the chief of staff has predicted that I will never again function with a semblance of normality but will probably have to spend the rest of my life in a wheelchair, hardly able to speak or to think, forever a helpless idiot who cannot possibly be cared for at home,

fortunately, I will fool them all, I am soon getting out of my bed, eating with Maria's help and reading the newspaper reasonably well, soon I am also able to follow the text of a book and walking along the corridors without needing help, even though a nurse is supporting me,

I start writing exercises, but my hands have turned stiff from rheumatism and my fingers will not obey, it is with great difficulty that I can now write my own name, and it is not much easier to go to the typewriter, time and again I hit a different key than the one I am aiming for, and when I try to read what I have written I must guess, and I often exclaim: "What did that idiot write!"

A couple of months after regaining consciousness I can now walk outside for half an hour at a time without any direct support, but I feel safer if someone comes along just in case, I can again read a difficult novel in Spanish and I can draft an article which I dictate to Maria, she will soon be a virtuoso on the newly acquired electronic typewriter and she types my manuscripts perfectly, with the exception of a few mistakes that can be traced to her Danish background,

however, it is proving more difficult than I had thought to put down the many strange dreams I have had during my two months of total unconsciousness, no matter how vivid those dreams seem to me they have a strange way of evaporating as soon as I try to catch them in words, I cannot possibly do them justice and I do not like weaving tales of fantasy around them so that they lose their authenticity,

at first I believe I have arrived by night train to Malmo and I am walking around without recognizing the city, and then I am sitting in a café which has opened early and while there, I begin talking with a Norwegian who wants me to come with him back home to Norway in his car,

we travel swiftly and I see nothing much except for cars rushing by, when we arrive at his house in a small coastal town I find that he is the owner of some kind of a ship's chandlery which, being a widower, he manages alone with the help of daughters Anita and Hjordis who are in their late teens, the man's name is Larsen and he is particularly keen on showing me some seals of a very rare species,

the seals are kept in a fenced-in basin where they are happily swimming around, and they immediately approach us to be petted on their heads, they are no bigger than half-grown cubs, they have a finely textured light-grey skin, as soft as fine gloves, their eyes are clear blue and twinkling with joy, and they come close to us to be stroked both by Larsen and by me between their dives into the water and their swift swims,

in the evening we sit nursing our whiskies, the girls are there to keep us company and Larsen is vivaciously telling us about his many adventures at sea before he went ashore for good, he asks his girls to sing something and they happily comply, they look at each other, expectantly, before they entertain us with the Norwegian national anthem, a song about a girl tending her cattle on the mountain meadows, and many other well-known Norwegian songs,

then it is bedtime and the girls say goodnight, I am shown to a chamber and sink into a bed where I immediately fall asleep, later, I am awakened by the two girls who have come into the room in their nightgowns and lie down next to me without further ado, one on each side, and there we are, chastely keeping each other company in the safety of closeness, in an unspoken unity of the bodies without anything else happening ❦

I *am sitting by my window, look-*
ing out on a typical street filled with people and vehicles and
then suddenly a train approaches, steaming, engines roaring,

at that very moment I am on
the train and two young Indian women in white saris come
walking by, carrying a washtub between them, they stop at
my side and tell me they are going to wash me, but I answer
that it is not necessary, I will soon get off, I am going to visit
a missionary station where I can take a bath, but the women
insist, and I must undress to my waist, right there in the
train, and let them have their way, and they happily proceed
to wash me and then they dry me off,

now I am sitting upstairs in a
café, together with two young women and a middle-aged
man with a greying moustache who turns out to be a younger
brother of the much acclaimed author William Faulkner, a
man I greatly admire, and he has himself written a book I
have read, I mention that I met his brother when he received
his Nobel prize in Stockholm but he says almost nothing,
just answers all the questions with the standard reply that he
was only a humble farmer from Mississippi, but that his
daughter, who was there with him, was a free-spirited college
girl who could answer any question,

the brother orders drinks for all
four of us, he is telling us stories about his deceased brother
who was also well known in his own home town, William
was awfully shy, did not like to speak to anyone, he preferred
to stay indoors writing but sometimes he went hunting, and
the hunt usually ended with his getting drunk, he had a spe-
cial feeling for the old city hall building,

then we are in a train, going
through Germany, through forests, monotonous to look at,
until I am suddenly alone and get off when the train stops,

it seems to me that I am in a
southern Italian town which I recognize, and I soon find

myself sitting on a terrace with a view of the sea, an orchestra starts playing fiery Italian music and the conductor comes up to me, bows to me while explaining that they are playing a piece composed by him, I thank him and give him a tip which he accepts without further ado, and now I have arrived in some remote part of China, ruled by a general, he is very lean and elegant in his uniform, with green leg wrappings, he has a small moustache, he has invited me to be his guest of honor, maybe he has mistaken me for someone else, I partake of an overwhelming feast, consisting of innumerable dishes which are brought in and taken out according to Chinese fashion,

the general proposes a toast to me and greets me with a speech of which I understand nothing, on either side of me I have a young Chinese beauty, breast bared and nipples big and red like cherries

I *leave the train at the station in* a major city, it might very well be Munich, and here I notice a passenger car of a train, it has been disconnected from the engine and stands by itself on a rail spur, I can see paintings through the windows as if the car were an art gallery, and this turns out to be the case,

the man comes out to greet me, he invites me to come in and see his exhibit and I am surprised at how much unusual art he is showing,

I immediately recognize a number of early paintings by Picasso, from his pink and blue periods, the warm, rich colors, the ascetic blues, the vivacious pinks, and the lifeless greys, scenes of youthful poverty and hunger,

I ask this man how he has acquired these rarities but he merely shrugs his shoulders and continues to look at other paintings, some that I recognize and others that I do not know if I have ever seen before,

the man tells me about his way of disseminating art, museums and ordinary galleries are not enough, it is easier to catch people's interest if the works of art are shown in unusual surroundings, like this train car which he moves to a new place after staying in one location for a while,

he is accompanied by his two daughters and helpers, I must have met them the previous evening, for when I wake up I am already acquainted with them, they come to me to give me an injection in the arm, they tell me they have been ordered to do so and I do not protest, I assume they must have good reasons and know what they are doing,

it seems I am staying in the railroad car for a couple of days, studying the works of art, and while there, I receive an injection from the amiable daughters every morning ◌

M*y present journeys differ from* all others I have made:

first of all, they are characterized by a total lack of planning and definite purpose, I have found that I am totally independent of travel funds and all kinds of papers establishing my identity, it is simply ideal travel without any cares and problems,

the movements themselves are rapid and effortless, I arrive from one place to the next, have no troubles with hotels or accommodations, everything is arranged by people I meet, I am given shelter and food, am taken care of by friendly and helpful persons, and I need not pay for anything, it is like travel in a better world, although it is otherwise quite like the usual one,

all of it appears totally natural to me, and I am not astonished at anything, do not worry about anything, accept the sudden moves as being quite natural, the journeys between very different places, often very long ones, take place rapidly and effortlessly, just as if I had lain down to sleep for a while and awakened in a new place,

nothing threatens me, I seem to be totally protected from accidents and pains of all kinds, if I believed in guardian angels I would have believed that I was accompanied by one, I never feel any fear or disquiet whatsoever, it is as if everything had been prepared and arranged by the most efficient travel bureau, independently of my wishes or intentions

T*he train carries me slowly north-*wards and finally stops at a station where I get out, nobody is to be seen on the platform but the station master who is just waving his red flag so that the train starts again, leaving silence and emptiness, particularly tangible so far up north in the vast forest lands,

then the station master comes up to me, wearing a red cap, just as I remember him from long ago, and I soon recognize him: it is none other than Jan Myrdal, an old acquaintance I have not seen for several years, and now he seems to have landed here, all the way up north, as a station master,

however, it does not particularly surprise me, nor that he extends his hand and welcomes me up there, as if he had been expecting my arrival,

it is fairly cold and we go up the stairs to the top floor of the station building where he has his home, which turns out to be well insulated by books covering the walls, mostly large volumes in solid bindings, apparently political and scientific literature,

I say that he seems to have ar-ranged things well for himself up north, and Jan nods with satisfaction and takes off the red cap, the moustache seems somewhat walrus-like and yellowish in the rosy face with the well-rounded cheeks, of course he looks a little older than before, but he does not seem to have aged conspicuously,

we speak of different things, of the world situation in which he is obviously just as interested as he used to be, I cannot clearly remember if we have had dif-ferences of opinions on many matters, but there is no conflict between us, Jan is in an excellent mood and more amiable than I can remember him to be,

it is as if all the great and volatile questions have been diminished by time and distance in space, there is no longer anything to debate, only a friendly exchange of thoughts, a truly heart-warming reunion up north, in the vast forests ❧

A gate, *a gate! I see it in front of* me, a gate in a high wall as around an old city, a gate that is still open, I can see that from a distance, a gate one must reach at the very last moment, before it is inexorably closed for the night or perhaps forever,

I hurry as much as I can, still running although I am losing my breath, my heart beats furiously in my chest, blood flows through my limbs so that my hands feel like stuffed gloves,

I probably will not make it in time, I despair about it but still continue my effort to the utmost, but if I do not arrive there before the gate is closed, I might just as well fall in front of it, and I am lying there as if dead, one arm still lifted to pound on the gate,

but in vain, meaningless, since the gate is of iron and there is not the smallest window or opening in the wall so that someone might see me ♪

At once the silence of the noon hour has grown pervasive, as if the entire world had become immobile, birds make no sound, the greenery stands as if varnished, congealed in the memory of the last shower, glittering like metal,

this moment that once was called that of Pan, when the spirit of wells and springs rose and was embodied, a moment that was both real and unreal, the hours of Panic terror when anything could happen, when all life was immobilized, rigid as if cast in metal, an alloy of iron and silver, when the drops of water were crystallized and became overly heavy without falling,

it is as if earth itself had stopped its movement and with it everything moving around it and given life by this movement,

then there is a faint whiff of wind, the leaves are freed from their petrification and move as if with innumerable fingers, as if playing a flute, still without any observable sound but already awakening a bird from its silence,

the world again assumes its place in the eternal circular motion, life regains its force beyond the Panic silence and immobility

It is a woman of mist but dense as if she were of flour, she is large but evasive, she cannot be embraced and caught,

she has no center, no womb, she is an undulation of masses of bellies and breasts,

she is not beautiful, nor ugly, it is impossible to form an idea about her, she is whatever you imagine her to be, neither more nor less,

she moves across the fields and the meadows like a cloud, as if dancing on innumerable small feet,

if she does have a mouth it is without lips to kiss, only a round hole seemingly opening and closing in the fog,

suddenly she also has an eye or a pair of eyes, shining blue but without form, not like zeroes or wells but like flowing wellsprings,

she is cold rather than warm, if you experience heat it comes from within yourself,

when you have chased her long enough without coming closer, you give up, tired as after lovemaking,

you sink down on the grass, and suddenly the sun shines 🜋

My dreams are of iron, so strong, so durable, but they soon begin to rust, eventually they fall off like flakes of rust and nothing is left of them, then I shift to dreams of dough so that I might bake and eat them, almost like bread,

suddenly, as I sit at the table in good company, I am nauseated, I do not even have time to stand up and run to the toilet before I spew out a snake that curls out of my mouth, one piece with each spasm, like a birth,

the snake lands in front of me, on the plate that is still empty, it is curled up, mottled, with a zigzag pattern on its back, more beautiful than a sausage and much longer,

the snake raises its head and opens its jaws as if to say something but at that moment, I faint and I do not hear it

I *am awakened by unusual clamor* and uproar, screeching tones from a barrel-organ, rhythmical thudding as from an endless passing train, screams and laughter from a mass of people crowding close to me,

I am sitting in a cage and the crowd is kept out by the iron bars, staring at me with curiosity and scorn as if I were a rare animal, pointing fingers at me, spitting in my direction,

they seem like visitors at a fair from far back, in old-fashioned clothes, apparently middle-class families with small children who are lifted up to see me better, and simpler folk, tradesmen and farmers it seems, and some of them carry walking sticks and are not above poking them into the cage to touch me or to hurt me and see how I react,

fortunately, I am covered with strong fur and the sticks do not cause me much harm, but I nevertheless fly into a rage and hit back so that the sticks are torn out of some of the hands, other sticks I snap at and catch them between my jaws, crush them,

this excites both me and the crowd, the screams and laughter grow increasingly violent, I leap against the bars of the cage and shake them threateningly, force the people to fall back, suddenly so that all are in danger of being trampled, women and children scream with fright,

I understand nothing, not why I am sitting there in the cage, not why the crowd is staring at me so intrusively,

I have not had time to be astonished at my fur and my strong jaws, nor by my belligerence and wild-mannered way of throwing myself at the bars of the cage,

and all the time this empty and regular thudding as from a train passing by, until suddenly a whistle cuts through the din and somebody cries into a megaphone: Ladies and gentlemen, time is up! Now you have seen the beast in human form!

and the crowd begins to disperse, leaves me alone in the cage, to consider my fate or to fall asleep again ॰

In a dream I imagine that I am gigantic, so large that common people are like small children by comparison, all houses are too small and I have to crawl into them as into narrow stalls, then back out when I want to move or stretch my back,

the food offered me is also much too insufficient, I would have needed hefty potfuls instead of these tiny morsels, I could have done work although tools become nothing but toys in my hands, I can tear down trees that are not too big, I can pull plows and farm machinery as well as a tractor,

it is worst when I am attracted to a woman, she can sit on my lap like a doll, but there can be no union with her, her kisses are nothing but a tickle at the corner of my mouth,

however, I am strongly aroused by seeing her naked and I look at her as I would at a small but very lifelike sculpture, of course also very much alive,

when my penis rises, she can climb up and sit astride it, she cannot do much more, her little tongue is more helpless than that of a kitten,

there is no other solution, I have to masturbate while we regard each other in longing infatuation, my sperm showers her like spilled cream, and she voluptuously rubs her entire body with it ~

T*hen, in another dream I imag*ine that I am very small, hardly as big as a baby compared to other adults, in spite of my being fully grown, a mature man,

apparently it is a case of the Gulliver syndrome with its exaggerated contrasts, the pendulum swinging to extremes, and after having been a giant, I am now a dwarf or smaller than a dwarf,

naturally, I am treated like a child, a very small but unusually advanced child who is surprising with his deep man's voice and the developed organ of a man, although miniaturized,

most of all, I am not taken seriously, whatever I say makes them laugh at me as if I were irresistibly comical in my precocity, and instead of letting me carry out any task whatsoever, they only want to play with me,

but other children, twice or more than twice my size, are suspicious of me and instead of playing normally with me they expose me to different kinds of maliciousness, although fortunately, I am surprisingly strong for my size and can defend myself fairly well,

there is also a woman who apparently falls in love with me, whether it is due to a delayed desire to play with dolls or to a dammed-up strong maternal instinct, perhaps she is ugly or too fat, but I do not notice,

to me, she is wonderful and utterly desirable, we sleep naked next to one another and I rest securely at her large bosom or climb all over her body like a little monkey, I can barely take her nipples in my mouth, gaping around them as around an apple, and I can easily stick my hand into her womb, up to the elbow,

I find no other relief for my own desire than to use a corner of her mouth, where my penis is

less filling than a cigarette and the membranes are almost too rough for me, particularly the tongue hurts me quite badly,
but nonetheless it is a loving relationship that is more satisfactory than most

I *have met imperceptible death,* without recognizing it, as an ever so rapidly passing pain, not a moment of suffocation or anxiety,

now I know that death is nothing once it has arrived, neither darkness nor visual impressions, just as if one never existed, a repose like an extinguished flame, leaving no trace,

there is no meaning to your having lived, it has meant nothing but itself, never anything beyond, as if you had never been, leaving neither disappointment nor bitterness,

why should man imagine a continued existence, and what would it be, if not a repetition of a more or less identical life and why, then, should it be repeated. . .

what reason is there to fear nothingness or to rejoice in it . . . the entire endless universe might exist under the same conditions, without a meaning beyond itself, life that is endlessly fired and extinguished, life shifting into death without any deeper transformation,

but we are bound to the concept that nothing has a meaning unless it is transformed into something else, a consequence of our incorrigible overestimation of ourselves ॽ

*A*nd where we are now floating in emptiness, how we long to return to our old world, how wonderful everything there seems to us, the old world that we so often scorned and condemned, the world now abandoned, burned out, devastated,

how is it possible that we will never return to it, that there is no longer anything to return to, how could all flowers, all pebbles and rocks cease to exist, all waters evaporate, even earth itself disappear . . .

how is it possible that a sun no longer rises over an earthly horizon, that no bird flies through the air, that the air itself has been devoured and nothing is left, nothing at all . . .

how is it possible that there is not even a speck of soot left of the big cities, that the animals in the glory of their fur and their feathers will never more be seen by a living eye, that nothing that can see or feel or think remains in existence . . .

where, then, dwells our own consciousness with its unending waiting, the unbearable pain of its memories, is it only a dying mirror image, a fading evening glow from the sun that has set ❧

*A*nd they ask you, one after the other: Well, do you believe in God now... you have been unconscious for two months, and if you haven't seen God in that time you are beyond hope,

here you have had your great opportunity, you could have born witness to His existence, of His presence in everything, but you have seen nothing, nothing at all, and you believe no more than you did earlier, this entire period of grace has been wasted on you, God gave you a chance but you did not grasp it, how can one be so hard-hearted, you will probably never again have an opportunity of this kind,

but you do not believe in God, why should He bother with you... you cannot remember that there was a place for a God in the world you left or that has returned from memory, which has ordered itself into varying patterns but where nothing is unknown or inexplicable,

so you have not been convinced of a life after this one, you have not had a glimpse of life beyond death, this might mean that you will never partake of the communion of eternal bliss, does it not bother you now, when you have been so close to death, that all you remember from the other side of life serves no purpose 🌀

One day, I discover that I have lost my handwriting, suddenly the hand and the pen no longer obey me, whatever my efforts, the writing is hardly legible,

actually, I always had difficulties writing by hand and my handwriting constantly changed as I was writing, but this day it happened: I cannot even write in the most infantile way, cannot shape a letter correctly and legibly,

laboriously, I try to draw the letters one by one but the result is not much better, I try with print type letters, upper case only, such as are preferred in anonymous letters, and it is reasonably legible but far from a handwriting,

if I had known runes or Babylonian cuneiforms I might have been able to use them, but I don't know them, and even under normal conditions Egyptian hieroglyphs would be too difficult for me, since it is writing that demands the skill of an artist,

no, none of the ways of writing of humanity are available to me now, as if the art of writing had distanced itself from me by many thousands of years, set me back to a past of ape-men or cave dwellers,

I sit down to wonder if this might be a temporary loss, a trap door that I happened to fall through, and if I might come up from it again, soon, regain my ability to write, however imperfect,

I also try to find out if other skills were lost at the same time, primarily that of reading, but that does not cause me any specific difficulties, I believe that I am also able to think, not better than usual but hardly worse, so it can hardly be a sudden breakdown of my sanity, as when a sandpit unexpectedly collapses,

it must be something that is only and mainly related to the hand, and that is more difficult to remedy, perhaps I could replace the hand one way or another, get a new hand, perhaps have a new hand from a dead person surgically attached, maybe even get an exquisite handwriting in the bargain, or, if it had to be a mechanical hand, it could be programmed to write well, if that were possible,

but it is not improbable that the reason is a deeper one, that a new hand would soon be just as unable to write as my present one is, perhaps the inability is due to some defect in myself, a defect that has always been there but has now become incurable,

of course I could type as I did before I was an adult, but I find that my hands fail me on the typewriter as well, I can only type one letter at a time, and I often make mistakes, so the difficulty must exist somewhere in myself

I *prefer to lie in a north-south* orientation when I sleep, with my head to the north and my feet to the south, across the direction of the earth's movement from west to east, so as not to feel like a projectile aimed toward the east, with either my head or my feet running ahead,

I lie with my head a little lower than my feet, since the earth slopes towards the North Pole, being a little pear-shaped with the pointed part towards the north, but this is of no practical importance and is impossible to experience,

I am very conscious of traveling, in three different ways and at very different speeds, and I have stored in my memory that the rotational speed of earth is approximately 240 meters a second where I am, but almost twice that at the equator,

that is already a speed far exceeding that of any gale, and if the layer of air were not a protection, everything would be blown away from the surface of the earth and be leveled to one single, terribly agitated ocean,

then there is the travel of earth around the sun, some thirty kilometers a second, considerably more than a thousand times faster than the speed of earth, and added to that is the movement of the solar system itself through the universe: combined, a journey through the cosmos so tremendous that it defies all imagination,

what a traveler man is even when he rests in his bed, I think to myself, amazed and trembling: to move on earth or in its atmosphere is slight by comparison,

one might just as well abstain from all movement, a snail crawl that is of no use, a piteousness, but if one travels to the equator, the speed of travel related to the rotation of the earth will be almost doubled, interesting enough but nothing at all when compared to the other two speeds of travel,

and still, one experiences neither one nor the other mode of travel but finds oneself unchangingly resting in one's bed while the sun passes to the east and adds days and nights to the year from season to season ♪

I *go to a street corner with heavy* traffic, stand still there or move a few steps back and forth, people rush past, usually without looking at me, almost as if I were a light post, some just miss running into me and give me an irritated look: why the hell is he standing there like an idiot!

in rhythm with the changes of the traffic light, people rush off across the street or stop, gather into a tight group waiting to rush on, for a little while I am part of this temporary group and at the moment, I am in nobody's way, but then the river of people flows past me again like water around a rock,

a policeman stops for a moment and looks at me, hesitantly, slightly disapprovingly and suspiciously, before he continues without saying anything, I also find myself observed by somebody or other who has stopped at some distance, observing, indecisive, perhaps ready to give me a secret sign or come up to me to say something,

if I stay there at the street corner long enough, somebody is sure to talk to me, ask me some question or make a request for something, perhaps offering me something, and probably, somebody with a camera will take a picture of me, openly or secretively,

I experience something like a cross draft between togetherness and loneliness, feel both that I belong and that I am an outsider, even more as a suspect person, dubious in the eyes of those who notice me at all, and I become increasingly embarrassed, cannot strike a natural position, nor move freely,

I am beginning to experience myself as shady or dishonest, somehow in pursuit of secret or criminal purposes, deserving to be arrested and indicted although I have done nothing more than deviating from traditional behavior, I have been a traffic obstruction at a street corner ঌ

The house is dark in the twilight of the summer night, either nobody is at home or else everybody is asleep, you stand there in the shelter of a leafy birch tree, quite certainly without being seen by anybody, you observe the house and have an impulse to go up to it, you only have to cross the lawn and don't have to step on the gravel walk leading up to the house, and thus you can approach the windows without being heard,

cautiously, you walk across the lawn and up to one of the windows, one that is slightly ajar, between curtains that are only halfway drawn you can see the interior of a room that is not completely dark, you can distinguish the furniture in there, a sofa with a couple of light-colored pillows, a sideboard with some shining object, nobody seems to be in the room and you hear no sound of people,

you move so that you can look in through the other window, you can distinguish a bed and the outlines of two people under some white cover, they seem to lie on their backs side by side with their faces turned upwards and vaguely recognizable as two oval shapes,

you do not see them making the slightest movement and you can hear no sound of their breathing, in their immobility they could just as well be dead and you suddenly believe that maybe they really are dead,

perhaps it is a couple who have committed suicide and you hesitate about what to do, if they really are dead it may be too late to save them and you are unwilling to intervene, you do not wish to be mixed up in a drama that does not concern you,

silently, you step away from the window and regain your position under the sheltering birch tree, actually you never left it but only imagined what you saw inside the house 🐚

A*s a child I seldom heard the* grownups telling each other of their dreams, they seemed to covet that which they had dreamed as fast secrets, and if they ever mentioned a dream it was shyly and with a soft voice, with words different from the ones they normally used, almost as Gospel,

what I did grasp was mostly fragmentary and for that reason particularly enticing, like a light that belonged fully neither to the day nor the night, like the light emanating from old, rotting tree trunks,

it was something happening in a borderline between real and unreal, outside of time and space, and often it had to do with the dead, often I heard them say: tonight, I dreamed about the dead, we will probably have a change of weather!

or else: I dreamed of Elna whom I haven't seen for so long, I wonder if she has died, perhaps we will know soon!

or the dream could be about places I did not know but where my father or mother were long ago, places and villages that immediately became real in my mind,

one was surrounded by a whole forest of tall junipers, in another there was a suite of steep waterfalls, another was a windy height with farms silhouetted against the sky, and another was a valley where one saw nothing but green slopes all around,

somewhere, there had been a sleepwalker who would climb the ridge of the roof in the middle of the night unless a tub full of water was placed by his bed, somewhere, a peddler had been killed and drowned in a tarn in the woods, from where one could hear him calling out in the night, but nobody ever said they had seen God or even Jesus, although they saw signs of the end of the world soon to come, mountain ash with berries large as apples, or a tremendous flock of lice wandering along a road,

there was also a rain of stars that set fire to the forests, and a band of horsemen rushing above, thundering like a storm and leaving everything afire behind them,

in the dreams, a different reality beckoned, one that was both enticing and terrifying, hiding that which was concealed and must not be mentioned in clear words ꙫ

O*utside the farm, there was the* village with other farms scattered at some distance, almost all of them painted red except for a couple of large buildings, one white, the other green, with echoing planked bridges across the village creek and a couple of walkways edged with dark spruce trees,

over there strangers lived, strangers with a different smell, who lived in a more modern time that was measured out by rhythmical wall clocks and was wound up with weights hanging in chains,

the main road to the church passed through the village and all who traveled there were seen on the church slope that seemed to be leaning and appeared light in the midst of the pine forest,

behind that the forest began, and the moors, the meandering creek and the half-overgrown lake, the cows who grazed without fences, knew the paths and followed them, and returned when it was milking time,

then there was the church village and the whole parish, the district and the county and the whole country, and it was on earth in the universe, below the sun, the moon, and the stars, with years carved into tree trunks without revealing if the world was actually old or still young ❧

Everybody on the farm sits in the great room at dusk, darkness falls slowly outside and the fire on the hearth has burned down to a heap of embers spreading their reddish glow throughout the room, everybody is quietly lost in his own thoughts or fantasies,

then the door suddenly slides open and a large black cat comes, looks ahead with shining eyes, almost glowing, and strides with determined steps across the floor, makes a quick jump up to the embers and lies down there, crouched as if to sleep but with its *eyes* open and burning white,

the deep silence continues and nobody moves, the cat stays by the embers and the heat seems not to bother it, it keeps staring straight ahead with the same red burning *eyes* as before,

after some time of continued silence, the cat rises from the embers and steps down to the floor, walks with rapid steps across the room and disappears through the crack of the door, while the glow dies on the hearth,

then somebody breaks the silence and says, slowly and quietly: old people say they have seen the black cat now and then, and it has always meant a death on the farm within a year, perhaps he brought us a message this time too, and perhaps it will be so, the others in the great room sit quietly, pondering what happened

T*hey are calling me back, my* ancestors in the soil call me back, I have gone too far away from them, they don't want me to disappear forever behind the waves of the grain fields and the blue shore of the forest,

they feel their forlornness in the soil as a betrayal, mine of them or theirs of me: what are they to do with this soil . . . how can it continue to blossom and bear harvests, how can the roots continue to nourish themselves from the old . . .

I must come back, come back! they cannot but believe that I do not fare well in the strangeness, the too far distance, where not even the sun is the same, far less the rains or the green, where leaves are sharply metallic and edged with sawteeth,

surely I must miss the horses, warm-blooded and affectionate, fish that let themselves be caught one by one, rock cleaving willingly under a sledgehammer, and berries to pick in the forest with one's fingers, paths that love the feet of the wanderer, water that is sky blue or night black,

they call me back, they shift between cajoling and threatening, but how can I return to the light that penetrates everything, the unceasing noise, return to images foreign like singing groups of pilgrims, or like hunters breaking camp in the morning . . .

but they are calling, continuing to call me back

I *dream that as a boy I stayed* on in the village back home, that I still walk around there like some village idiot, held in contempt by all, followed by children who point their fingers at me and cry insults at me, I have not aged much, but I have grown taller than the others, I walk with my head bent down so as not to stand out too much, my clothing is wretched, and I notice that I smell bad, too,

and still, I know that I carry within me something that has never fully blossomed, I could have become someone distinguished instead of staying in the village, I don't know what I would have done, but I feel it within me and it is my greatest pain at the same time as it is my secret joy ♋

I*t occurs to me that I want to shout,* to scream full-throatedly, without using words, only sounds, just as a dog howls or a cow stands by herself in the middle of a field, mooing without any consideration of whether she is heard or not, but I cannot easily shout like that in my dwelling in the city, I must get to a forest, alone,

I ride a bus as far as it goes, then I walk into the forest as far as I have the energy to go, then I sit down to rest on the trunk of a fallen tree,

after a while, I stand up and start shouting, I send out long calls, wordless but welling out of me as if to liberate me, as if I were a howling animal, a being that can only produce loud screams or wails,

I listen for the echo of my own voice in the forest without recognizing it as being my own, and I feel free, as if something had broken loose inside me, something age-old and too long pushed aside, something denied that has waited within me and now bursts out with full force, the expression of a drive as basic as hunger or thirst, a need to shout without end, without inhibitions, without consideration of anything,

I feel the air fill my lungs with new freshness, I breathe deeper, feel stronger and strangely renewed, as if I have discovered, for the first time, a new and unknown facet of myself, as if I have come closer to my origin and reached a deeper being within myself,

I return from the forest and take the bus back home, a different person than the one who went out ❧

I *feel an itching between my toes,* there is also a weak pounding in them, like a pulse, and when I look at my feet I see that two green saplings have emerged between the toes,

I now begin to wonder what is going to happen to these saplings, will they shoot up, maybe develop into small trees growing upwards along my legs, or will they become vines, spreading out green and succulent...

I wonder what I should do with these growths, will I have to water them and tend them, perhaps unable to rise or go out, or put on my clothes, will I have to remain naked, or is it enough that my feet are bare, will I still have to put on some kind of shoes to protect the plants without preventing their growth...

while I am pondering all this, I look down at my toes again and find that the green shoots have disappeared, they seem to have been nothing but a mirage, and I feel relief but at the same time happiness, for I take the green shoots that I saw between my toes as an omen: a good sign that life continues to grow inside me

I*t hurts when buds are bursting,*
the poet says, but she is the one feeling the pain, not the buds,
it is unreasonable to expect that
nature should feel anything of the suffering it is subjected to
or causes itself, only you, regarding nature and identifying
with it, experience a feeling, be it pain or pleasure,
you suffer seeing the flowers of
spring force their way up from the still cold soil, you grieve
for their brief life before they begin to wither and die, all their
efforts in vain and meaningless, so short a time of bloom and
beauty before they die and disappear again,
you suffer with autumn for its
merciless sacrifices, the masses of leaves offered to frost and
storms, fruits brought forth with effort only to fall to the
ground and rot unless an animal or a human finds them and
devours them,
nature is ignorant of itself, feels
and senses nothing, has no will or ambition, merely follows
its predetermined path, fulfills its destiny, an enormous sac-
erdotal system without meaning, what man would call a programmed process followed without mercy,
the higher animals, even the
most insignificant creatures, have a short consciousness of
some kind of existence, be it one of joy or one of pain,
but as for the rest, although it
all has some kind of existence, it is not conscious of it ᘛ

*B*lacksmiths and spinning women, blacksmiths and spinning women, our predecessors in the flickering light of tar torches, sledgehammers singing against the anvil, turning spindles whirring under the eyes, the taste of iron black and red against the tongue, the fingertip feeling of oily but nevertheless rough wool,

iron that banished evil and shed the black blood of the enemy, the thread entering the weave to be glued together into cloth, shiny as frog spittle and almost watertight, weapons and weaves to protect against nakedness, against bareness and cold, the naked warrior so inferior to the one in clothing, tones entering the strings of the harp and sounding as if plucked by fingers out of the skies,

artful smithwork, iron chastised and formed into flower stalk and snake body, the animal that followed man, defeated and terrifying, tulip mouths and dragon jaws, the cock on the tower spire, the weathervane at the gable, the rosebush pattern before the window, iron roses on the bedstead, the sleigh with flower garlands in red,

all painted as if with fire and soot, the sticky white, the sooty black, scythe edges and swallows, the arrow concept of death carried by the dream of escape,

the dead man resting in the moor, straight in his homespun, the woman still with the noose around her neck after a thousand years and her chest with a pole through her heart, fear shackled in sun crosses of iron

T*he quarry is truly terrifying,*
crime against the rock, murderous attack on the rock,

the rock as a giant animal crouched in the earth with its hardened flesh of stone, with rifts and memories of pain,

the immense stone body of the subterranean rock, this flesh that never rots or devours itself, that breathes so slowly that cities are built and destroyed in the meantime,

the rock now penetrated by water-cooled steel drills, smoking and rattling like devils rattling their teeth in the midst of hell's heat, to be torn to pieces by the foul-smelling dynamite, this dough grey as a murderer's brains, without a drop of blood, without the slightest scream or moan, the life of the rock held back for a hundred million years,

the men work in the quarry retaining the character of slaves, grey with stone dust, coughing grey saliva with drops of blood, reddish flowers upon the rock,

the men in their half-petrified gloves, the stone penetrating into the body, making it heavier, more immobile, until it dies as its own statue,

the drill steel is sharpened over fire hissing like a snake and flaming in gluttonous rage, the work sheds grey as if covered with elephant skin, the cranes with blocks of stone in their jaws are squeaking angrily, the quarry is the belly of a giant torn open with the entrails torn to pieces, it is the terrifying murder of a sleeping innocent, on whose body our existence is resting,

all wood looks chewed as if large animals had been eating of it, chewing it and trying in vain to swallow it before leaving again 🌀

I *had never before imagined nuns* in wood-white clogs and hand-knitted black wool stockings held up, albeit not very well, by garters below their knees, these knees seen by nobody, maybe not even by themselves since they bathe dressed in coarse linens reaching to their feet, their bodies forbidden and unknown to themselves,

nuns with faces naked as bared bottoms, it seems indecent to regard them closely, faces with an innocent little streak of shadow for a moustache above the mouth, with fresh skin like apples in the shade and with small red pimples, eyes thinly edged with pale red and small yellow scales,

these mouths had been victorious in battle with themselves, long since used to not opening too wide, neither to food nor to drink, to spoon nor to fork, nor for words, and most of all, not for a smile or a laugh,

nuns looking like forgotten but endlessly waiting brides, followed by the sudden clatter of clogs on wooden floors or stone floors, as if noble guests had arrived or a fire had broken out,

nuns girlish in a flock, girl-women, girl-grannies, young as tree trunks below the bark, anticipating wonders sparking in their eyes, with hips swelling as if pregnant with a momentous promise, this in a distant convent in the pine forest, among squirrels and woodpeckers, with a dirt road fighting the grass, with light clouds passing and passing, the pure Lamb of God with whitewashed wool,

all suddenly so self-evident although never before considered, I nothing but a distracted visitor surrounded by the aura of his sins, with a scent of markets and gasoline: a meeting where we barely touch one another and which has no purpose, one that merely leaves a feeling of echoing emptiness and sadness

You can see flocks of birds against the spring sky, pollen edges the riverbanks with yellow, a silken black bird with wheat-colored beak follows the shore-lines and sings like a master of the treetops, also showing the direction of the wind,

there are the tall ones, the blond and reddish ones, with eyes blue as lakes and sky, hands with calloused grips and hair like sparse grain on the body,

they are like gods singed by fire, grandiose, bragging, power-charged, urinating like stallions, contemptuous of the renegades who flocked to the pale god or to Ulfila, for them rather skulls of horses carried on lances, tails of horses fluttering in the wind between tents of skins and sails of skins,

the oars are smeared with honey so as not to squeak and creak, smoke gives taste and smell to man and follows him like the fresh tar and the white birch bark around the dwellings with groups of swine and poultry, there are rotating grindstones and stone mills already invent-ed and brought along for the journey,

the art of smithing is half secret, its masters living in caves, at hearths with fire, shrunken to dwarfs and enlarged to giants, strings are strung between bows of trees, with harmonies plucked by the wind like wildflowers, fire lives in the flint, knife-sharp, and attracts lightning,

the shores of the sea yield amber that its gall-green stomachs cannot digest, like petrified sun-shine from the darkness of depth, for ornaments between women's breasts and on wrists, with a fly caught in the amber as a small miracle to gaze upon in a streak of sun that shines through the fingers making them wine red,

the long boats are buried in earth with their chieftains to never more tempt them to break up and travel, the settled ones anchored by rocks and tree trunks

T*he plain seems almost like a* desert, with sparse grass in the sand, and a wagon covered with a vault of sailcloth as in the Old West is seen traveling away, towards the sharply cut, harshly blue mountains,

there seems to be neither a draft animal nor a driver, unless they are hidden beneath the sailcloth, but a woman is walking in the opposite direction and will shortly meet the wagon,

apparently, the woman is an elegant lady in hat and gloves, in high-heeled shoes, with a sunflower-yellow parasol held high above her, a strangely misplaced or incredible person in this landscape,

it seems like an absurd encounter arranged by the artist who has also placed a lone tree against the horizon, shaped with a trunk like the high and slender neck of a woman, and with a leafy crown-like flowing hair, or densely rising smoke ✍

During *the desert journey we stay* overnight in some ruins with walls rising from the sand drift and protecting us against the hyenas whose howls are heard approaching from out in the darkness, no roof protects against the night sky with its overwhelming multitude of stars, they hang there threatening and intrusive like large, heavy, shining drops ready to fall,

the darkness is velvety soft but the cold eventually increases and, with innumerable fine needles, it penetrates the blankets where a smell of sheep remains,

I awaken needing to urinate, hesitate to go outside into the nudity of the desert night, do it stealthily in a corner, covering it over with sand like an animal that does not want to leave its scent,

I awaken bathed in perspiration in the invading early sunshine and to my surprise, I hear the buzzing of flies, which have appeared out of nowhere in the midst of the desert

A*fter passing a block house, long* since deserted and without gates, its unpainted wood overgrown with silver grey moss, I leave the forest behind and come out onto a mesa which is truly flat as a table and extending in all directions, covered with a fresh green cloth and space for innumerable guests,

but there are only a few people, the feast has not yet started and may not even be planned as yet, a couple of men in large hats shaped like pagodas make all of the donkeys below them disappear except for the ears, some women with skirts to their feet walk back and forth, barefoot, twirling spindles in their hands, spin the silky, fine wool of the protected animals of the mountains,

a church has large round blue eyes instead of windows, and the door is so low that one has to enter on one's knees, it creates a feeling of humility and of passing through a womb,

the interior is dominated by a gypsum madonna, brightly painted as a prostitute, for the poorest ones, in front of her some drooping cloth flowers in a waterless vase, the child in her arms looks sickly swollen with all the signs of suffering from dropsy, nevertheless the child smiles grandly and shows a full set of sharp teeth of mirror glass,

then there is a crowded village, draped in dust as in eternal fog, with many wells, open, without lids, but not particularly deep and with no water in them, filled with coiled snakes fed with the remains of chickens left by guests at the inn,

skeletons of men rest on shelves of stone, gracefully stretched out though with nothing but the rock to lean their skulls against, worn saddles are hung in the sparse, uncared-for trees where the leaves seem to be numbered and carelessly stitched on,

after, I enjoy boarding a raft with an outboard motor which starts out briskly on the river of no return, which is what its Spanish name means: el Rio sin Retorno ᴼ

I *imagine it could have happened* like this: as when a train rushing forward suddenly dives into the depths together with an old stone bridge, in this way they could have sensed the earthquake that made the house collapse over them and surround them with sudden darkness,

it was the young couple surprised in bed just as they were lying there naked, ready for the act of love, clinging close to each other in fear, and finding that they were still alive and unharmed but enclosed by total darkness,

they could move in the bed but not much more, in all directions their groping limbs met broken walls, rough surfaces of wood or stone, while they heard water running as from a half-open faucet, otherwise silence deep as death,

the air was suffocating and full of dust that penetrated into their mouths, dried them out and took away all saliva, reached down into their lungs and made them cough and gasp,

they could not even rise halfway, they let each other loose and turned in different directions, then they embraced each other again, body against body, as if to comfort one another that they were still alive,

they would have had enough space and more than enough time to make love, for which there had not been time before the quake, but their lust was dissolved and did not return, the fear of death and the anguish attacked them and made their hearts beat violently,

the miracle that they were alive was not enough, they were far from saved, the worst could still be coming, they listened in vain for any sounds, for any sign of people surviving, but nothing, only a silence as in the grave,

they realized that they were buried alive and that it was uncertain whether they would be found while they were still alive, perhaps another quake would crush them or a tidal wave surge up and drown them, or fire burn them alive,

all kinds of fears shot through them again and again and left them in deep uncertainty, the woman wept in the arms of the man and he began to sob as well, until they realized that crying was meaningless and they no longer found comfort in one another,

the life of their bodies no longer had a meaning, neither that of the other or one's own, they began to feel that it was a mockery, after a while that it was revolting, in the stench of urine and feces that they could not hold back,

the cold slowly stole in over them together with hunger and thirst, they lay there close to each other, shaking, the thought of merely a splash of water pained them the most, followed by the shrieking emptiness and nausea of hunger,

if they tried to talk, everything turned into wheezing, nor did they have any words left, nothing to say, nothing but a wordless moaning now and then,

a desire to bite each other's limbs came over them, a desire for flesh and blood, dimly, it occurred to them that they could eat of one another and survive longer, resist hunger and cold better,

they lost all concept of time, of day and night, everything was only darkness and eternity, all events had stopped, they were only faintly surprised that it could take so long to die, that it was so difficult, and almost without being aware of it, they began to bite each other's limbs and suck the blood,

when they were finally dug out of the ruins, they were unconscious, with congealed blood around their mouths, and when they returned to life, they no longer felt any love for one another, only an irresistible aversion,

        but now, I say now, it does not have to be like that, the couple that has returned to life after being so close to death may find each other again, may be closer to each other than ever, in a common gratitude for the return of life after having consumed flesh and blood of one another, as if partaking of a new kind of sacrament

T*he high-rise hotel was built by* Japanese and when, after years of work, they completed the imposing building and returned to their own country, a rumor began to spread that a couple of the Japanese had remained in the building, in hiding somewhere, but nobody was ever certain of having seen them, and nobody knew where in the building they might be,

there were those who maintained that they had seen them, met them on a staircase or glimpsed them in an elevator, but they always suddenly disappeared again, and nobody knows where they might have gone,

the hotel has turned one year old and two years old, and it is still believed that the Japanese are there, but nobody can prove it or discover where they are in the building, one assumes that they have artfully and ingeniously built themselves into the hotel, that they live somewhere in one or several rooms that nobody has succeeded in discovering,

nor does anyone know how they can still live in this secret hiding place, as far as it is known nobody has seen them go out or provide themselves with food and other supplies, although there are rumors that things disappear from the kitchen now and then, but nobody has seen the Japanese there, and nobody can prove anything,

people speculate that they might have secured vast stores of food and can continue to live walled in, in their secret hiding place, not needing to go out, nor desiring to do so,

eventually, a mystical rumor is created that the two Japanese are not alive but that they have been dead all the time, that they have followed an old Japanese tradition and walled themselves into the building alive and now lie there as mummies joined with the life's work they left behind, proudly part of the monument they secretly made for themselves and did not want to survive, perhaps the secret of the Japanese will never be disclosed but the legend of their living death in the hotel will survive ⟨6⟩

A*lone in the wilderness you shed*
no tears, the animal has entered you unnoticed, without
laughter or crying, staring straight into Fate,

your joy can turn against you like
a crushing argument, and like a gleaming axe it can cut a scar
of warning into the alabaster of your hip,

if you walk backwards down a
flight of stairs you can feel the hidden eye in the back of your
head moving, close to awakening from its long sleep,

when you look into the eyes of a
dead animal, you can distinguish a small cross of light in each
eye and behind it, the dark silhouette of a city in ruins,

white hail bouncing off a naked
statue may leave small, dark dots like a disease attacking,

the wheel of a wheelbarrow rolling
across the palm of a hand leaves an unforgettable memory, and
a cat run over by a bicycle never overcomes its astonishment,

the poplar is dressed in a long
dress, like a greening bride where only the waist is difficult
to find,

there are statues that have been
standing so long that their legs have varicose veins, almost as
if grapes were bursting out of their calves,

there are handshakes that echo
in your ears long afterwards, as if you have just sold your soul
or at least your most beautiful horse

It is the *usual old illusion: piano* notes through an open window where an airy curtain is fluttering, and I stop there under the tree on the boulevard in the large-leafed shadow, a listening wanderer in the evening, half invisible,

the curtain moves softly out and in as if breathing, the music flows out in waves, in cascades, as crystal rain, a string of tone pearls, rhythmically tied together,

it may be a Viennese waltz or a piece by Chopin, softly rocking waves of the Danube or the hoofbeats of cavalry storming forward, ladies floating around in wide skirts, gold-embroidered hussars with wasp waists,

I imagine a young mother playing for her sick child, already half alone in her pain, still soaring upwards jubilantly, like a wounded lark,

naturally, it could also be a man playing, young or old, filled by his hopes or by ascending memories, while his life's companion is listening, recently married to the man or aged together with him,

but I can hardly believe anything other than that eyes in there look towards the open window and follow the waving movements of the curtain which resemble breezes in a sail, the house sailing away through the world,

and as long as this beautiful illusion remains somewhere, all is not lost ♪

A storm is rising, a storm is rising!
Hurry, the storm is already here! close the windows, hold on to
the curtains so that they do not tear themselves away, fast! cut
an armful of roses before they are torn apart and swirl away!

hurry out for the freshly washed
clothes hanging to dry before they are filled by the wind as
sails, free themselves and sail into the air!

chase the chickens indoors so that
they will not be taken away like a whorl of snow, close the
swinging barn door but be careful so that it does not knock
you down with a terribly forceful cuff on the ear!

hear the growing roar that the
storm drives ahead of itself, like a cattle herd in panic! see
how the trees resist, dig in with their roots and flex their
branches as a boxer flexes his arms; see how the sky cools and
sharpens its blueness, polished like the blade of a knife!

kill the fire before the storm sows
the sparks, gather in here, behind locked double doors, waiting for the doings of the vicious wind that howls and foams
like a lunatic ༅

O*nly one who has traveled in* deserts knows what greenery means, only one who has lost his way in the sea of sand knows what water means,

after the suffocating grip of heat around the throat, cold advances like a rug of nails, cries are meaningless and nobody sees a waving hand, a man may fall like a tree trunk without a crown, his blood dried to a powder like the smoky dust of a crushed brick,

the palm trees are the trees of draught half-petrified into minerals, the snake is a miracle, the lonely eel of the sand sea, and the gazelles are ghosts traveling raised off the ground, one may find blind fish following the water from subterranean lakes and one may chew one's jaws out of joint on the tough meat of camels, these muscles so tightly packed with weariness,

time is astronomical or canceled as if on a natural scale map, it only begins or ends where the desert ends, evaporated oceans have left frightening abysses, depths as if mountains had been torn away from there and become moons in space, ruins of dead forests stand like columns of burned-out palaces, thickets of crackling skeletons have been left by animal herds that died,

life once wandered from the marshes to the desert, and maybe the last humans will disappear in deserts, with history left behind like an empty and withered tent of leaves, all memories merely a disappearing puff of smoke on the horizon

*A*shes rise from the embers and fall over us like fine flour, dry-tasting, drier than the tongues of the birds,

the dangers have snapped at our heels like angry dogs but have been unable to tear the flesh from our legs,

danger makes our steps elastic, uncertainty burns like alcohol in the blood, preparations against fatigue and despair, behind us the endless crowds of the dead mumble and complain, like an ocean of waves as dense as treetops in the forest,

as the armies of Alexander waded through high wormwood in the Mesopotamian desert and were intoxicated by its scent without feeling its bitterness,

we wade through the heather of these highland slopes, the heather that has burned and been resurrected, white and red, white and red as milk and wine,

sunset crowns the days with a flaming tiara of gold and deep red like a celestial clock face bursting into flame,

the shadows are our mantles with a darkness of compressed colors, each stone against which we rest has its forehead and might think as we do ◝

A stone bridge leads across to a small island along the coast of the Black Sea, and this island is bristling with church towers like a hedgehog, hundreds of churches are crowding it side by side within the old ring-wall,

the churches seem to have once fled there from the mainland, escaping enemies and pursuers, like women escaping invading armies, women who seem to remain in the churches as ghosts around the walls,

they are byzantine, elongated like evening shadows with extended, strangely dark faces, like icons blackened by incense or the flames of wax candles, against the background of gold like eternalized sunsets,

much gold from the mainland has been collected there over the centuries, gold treasures have illuminated the churches and been buried in the ground during times of disaster, so the mayor tells the visiting strangers,

he is a small man, dressed in black and barefoot in his sandals, his shirt open at the neck, and as gifts to the visitors he hands out small clay figures, not larger than fitting into the palm of a hand,

simultaneously, the bells are ringing in many of the church towers and a line of wedding trains moves over the stone bridge, on foot, in horse-drawn carriages or automobiles, preceded by accordion players and dancing youths who scatter flowers around them, a tapping of feet moves over the ancient cobblestones and the scattered flowers are amassed to a living carpet in the many different colors of early summer:

it is a meeting between widely separated times that for a short while attempt to fuse with one another ❧

These Gothic churches are decorated as stunning jewelry boxes, as imitations of ice caverns with stalactites, with bundles of upwardly aiming lines and pointed vaults,

what artful embroideries in stone, shaped into forest thickets with spirals of vines, with clusters of roses, grapes, and fruits, with bared hearts sending out rays like lightnings,

the madonnas and the angels so well-fed and chubby, unbaked white, with obliquely cut Asiatic eye slits below heavily arched eyebrows, so at home in their bodies and so sure of their importance,

the men in heavy wooden mantles and with beards of lathe-turned spiral locks combed into deep waves, grasping stone-like books that seem impossible to read or even to open, some of them with a lamb on a wooden board under the arm,

all victorious, autocratic, even the martyrs triumphant in their pains and the blood flowing copiously from the side of the Savior

Largely, *the deserts have already been rendered impassable* by accumulations of throwaway overproduction, all the world's things that have become useless, commodities that no longer pay off, miniatures that take up too much space, mirrors that have fallen hopelessly in love with waterfalls,

all these well-known things that advertising has tired of, that can rouse no interest even in the nudest of women, the moss that has covered the breasts of stainless steel, the foam rubber that has become foam, as worthless as that at the seashore, all limbs that have been successfully replaced with artificial limbs, adjustable phalli of appropriately hard rubber, mechanical toothbrushes to exert soft violence on rows of teeth, and dentures that chew the food several hours in advance,

soon, no deserts will be enough for this overwhelming production, one must take it to the sea, but the sea soon threatens to flood a number of large cities and the last wheat fields, the mud hardens and nothing more sinks into its insignificant depth, the whirls of quicksand have stopped like malfunctioning meat grinders, the tornadoes bring along sand to fill discarded hats,

ferrets live in ladies' shoes that they carry along on their backs during their wanderings, the snails never complete their conventions where they look like drifts of broken asphalt, loudspeakers facing downwards turn only to roots that are already nonexistent, signs cry out for help where they are drowning in sand, the beams of floodlights are petrified into conical tents, assembly-line razors cut the straws of grass before they have time to grow, but suddenly, the liberating cry is heard: The excavators are coming!

I*f all greenness should perish, then*
the flesh might also cease flourishing around the human
skeleton, without greenness the eyes will soon be blinded by
the whiteness of metals and the stony blue of space,

once upon a time greenness came
marching into the world, nobody knew from where, greenness came slowly and thoughtfully, almost creeping, licking
with fine little tongues of grass,

the trees came wandering like in-
fantry body next to body, their leafy crowns assimilated the
winds and clothed their nakedness, the birds followed the
greenness and themselves seemed covered with leaves,

the first humans lived like naked
lizards in the trees, feared the ground and the fire, they were
fast but nevertheless easy for larger animals to catch and eat,
making insignificant cracking sounds between their jaws

It was almost impossible to truly remember or imagine cold, but as soon as one met it, one immediately recognized it, surely that's what it was, whitish grey, taciturn and barren, so difficult to disregard and get used to,

cold is called clean and brisk but was dull and gave a headache, even the houses could feel the cold and became brittle, the trees seemed to turn into glass and broke rather than bent, water became window-panes on the ground before it solidified into shapes of grey-ish white porcelain,

the ground hardened like iron and the iron seemed to burn of cold, the smoke hesitated when facing the cold skies and pretended to be trees of cotton, sound displayed its speed to the naked eye as both marked a woodcutter from a distance,

cold went as long shawls of frost through the rooms, felt its way under the bedcovers, looked in through the keyholes, tarried even in woolen garments before allowing itself to be chased away, turned up as a waiting guest at a funeral in black and white,

leaves detached themselves and fell hard as metal, forgotten roses blackened in terror, candle flames were shivering, small birds ruffled up to double their own size to be frightening or to encourage themselves,

cold was tightfisted but nevertheless lavish with itself when that was to be so, cold, so intrusive and everpresent, an invisible holy ghost of rigidity,

but why was it so hard to remember afterwards, as if it took away even the memory of itself when it disappeared, without a trace like a ghost, disembodied, without substance, without intention and will, ignorant of itself, and still, still ༕

The drop of water frees itself from the thickening mass of the rain cloud and begins to fall, it forms itself accordingly due to its own weight and to the resistance it meets in the air, it ceases to be spherically round and is somewhat elongated, point down,

when you see the drop hit the windowpane in front of you, its fall is interrupted with a sound that is half a clink and half a thud, it begins to stretch itself in the slower and almost hesitant fall downwards when it meets the resistance of the glass and becomes a flowing motion,

you can see how the drop is thinned out and appears more and more as a narrow line on the pane before it disappears below the edge of the window and leaves only a pale trace of water down the glass,

the short existence of the water droplet has passed, and it becomes part of the rain water that flows in ever denser streaks down the glass and joins the multitude of rain drops that reach the ground below the window,

you have experienced some of the brief lifespan of the rain drop, and the memory of it remains in your vision while you still hear the clink of its impact on the window, with a tone that seems to have come from high up in the sky

*W*hat good does it do to caress an ocean, apart from the feelings it gives you . . .

only the palm of your hand touches lightly or brushes against a water surface that is an infinitesimal part of even the smallest of oceans,

the palm of your hand becomes wet, the water surface slightly disturbed, but there is no understanding of the underlying feeling,

the caress is in vain, wasted, it does not feel right in the hand, nor against the water surface,

better then, that in your love of the ocean, you throw your entire body into the water, swim forth in it as long as you can, caress the water with all your surfaces and with all your powers,

perhaps the ocean still will not understand your good intentions but merely waits for you to drown, something that might be the corresponding expression of the ocean's love, of which you can endure very little, being a man ♪

T*he cloud that I study is vast as a* respectable field and may seem fairly recently plowed, not unlike a field prepared for seeding but not yet sown.

the cloud is woolly along its edges and gives me a taste of coarse farm homespun, I cannot see the cloud move, but nevertheless it is in a different position although I only averted my eyes for a short while, it moves flowingly as if the sky were water supporting it, and I can sense or believe that I sense its weight over me, almost as if it were a cap, heavy after being drenched by a shower,

the cloud has neither body nor soul but can give an impression of having both,

it must happen that migrating birds travel through a cloud, large and heavy birds lowering themselves out of the cloud with pearls of water on their feathers, birds that might be calling out to each other inside the cloud so as not to lose one another, and their trumpeting sounds take on a tone of veiled oboes or water organs,

however, one cannot travel with a cloud, it either floats away from you or remains behind, the speed of the cloud is very difficult to judge, it may be faster than a horse running swiftly, but it may also move slowly, almost like a snail in half-high grass or a flock of geese slowly waddling away,

but unlike many others who travel, the cloud will always arrive, or else it tires of the effort and lies down to rest above a forest or a plain where it slowly descends as a quiet rain throughout the night ⋖

F*ear the sun, fear its fury from* which we are spared only by distance,

hardly a second can you bear looking into its glow when it sinks towards night, black suns surround you as if seeking your blindness until you see all suns merely as needle stings through the darkness,

only you cannot hear their roar, their uninterrupted explosions that are devoured by the distances, the merciful distances, the blessed distances from the unbearable, the unfathomable, forces that constantly destroy themselves for billions of years, beyond all time, beyond every imaginable space,

it is the vertigo, the annihilation, the absolute darkness or the absolute light, both equally unfathomable, and then the secret thought that maybe, after all, everything may not exist, is nothing but imagination, a nightmare of humanity

W*ho dares declare his love to the*
sun, who can have any relationship with the sun . . . it is too
enormous and overwhelming, we cannot even look at it with
our eyes open without being immediately blinded,

the sun is the master of space, the
ruler of our universe, the roaring lion in the high which is at
the same time the deep, it must be utterly inconsequential to
the sun whether our small planet exists or not, the sun is too
immense to share any of our troubles,

the existence of the sun could be
imagined as an unending suffering rather than as some kind of
bliss, it does tear itself apart constantly in a rage that never
solidifies, it is an expression of violent wrath rather than of
lovingness,

the sun is so far from everything
human that it seems like a bleeding taunt that human existence depends on it, what are we with our earth but red or
blue lice in the colorless darkness of the heavenly blanket, if
we burned in a moment there would be no more of a crackling than if a louse were crushed,

the sun is one single flaming rebel-
lion, the truly ongong revolution, the ultimate law of self-
destruction,

the sun has often been worshipped
as a god and perhaps it is the greatest fathomable or unfathomable symbol of god, a god who creates and destroys himself without pause while eternity turns around itself, the sun
has certainly sacrificed no son to save us, it answers all our
questions only with its flaming laughter,

how can we imagine any other
relationship to the sun than this our blind and circumstantial
dependency,

the sun owes us nothing and we
cannot expect anything from it, it does not know what it has
created, we are the abandoned children of coincidence in the
unending, meaningless emptiness

There are days with a certain light: the landscape no longer resembles a painting but a drawing, with bold and sparse lines, contours as of water and shadow, silver blackness and lines drawn as by the flight of swallows, straight until they unexpectedly bend into curves and angles,

the landscape is like a skeleton without flesh, bone-hard and white, only the beginning of a body, the skeleton like a harp singing with tones of bone, lines that enjoy themselves, young and flexible but almost disembodied, contours to fill out, unfulfilled promises,

divided between summer people and winter people we lead two kinds of life, halves that are barely joined into a unit, with stressful readjustments between red and white, sun and snow, dressed in straw like old-fashioned water pumps in the countryside, the straw of summer that becomes the clothing of winter,

the planter is the green man who has succeeded the forester with authority, moose as a hazard for motor traffic is no longer a matter of his concern, nor are wild geese spending the night on the roofs of deserted railroad stations,

the new tyrannosauri break loose and devour the forest, dig deep furrows in the earth and leave the rocks naked as moons shining on the steep slopes, the spoons of the lake filled with molten lead leave their reeds rusty, but where are the moose to drink, where are the deer to flee . . .

but there are such rich flowers around the deserted train tracks, navvy roses, navvy roses! and where the view is opened from the window of a compartment you can see villages slide into the river and disappear while roving smoke seeks its lost chimneys ✑

Y*ou are sitting there, reading in* the lamplight while the springtime evening darkens outside, the text of the book moves through your consciousness at the same time as you are semiconscious of existing in another plane, you are an infinitesimal point in the boundlessness beginning outside the circle of lamplight,

your two consciousnesses meet without fusing, the point where you are has an undefined relationship both with the consciousness which understands the text of the book and with the consciousness of yourself as a reader,

you are reading a tale of ancient Egypt and the time ruling there is totally different from your own time as a reader, you are conscious of the fact that as a reader, you are simultaneously part of both eras, one kind of time existing in the book and another time in your own consciousness,

the two times pass independently of one another as two courses of events on totally different planes, what has happened in ancient Egypt happens there and then while something different happens in your own time as a reader, they are two totally different chains of events but nevertheless simultaneous, without engaging one another or in any way fusing,

and outside the circumference of your consciousness there is yet another time, that of the spring night outdoors, a time belonging to the sky above the night and the infinity reaching beyond it, perhaps there exists a consciousness that we do not know and cannot imagine,

thus the reader is never alone, his own consciousness is only a connecting point between different events and eras, he is at the center of an unfathomable mystery without being truly conscious of it ༂

I *finally discovered that I was a* night person, long enough was I pained by the endless wearying days, the general rushing forward in a crowd, this forced behavior resembling that of everybody else or most others, since there were indeed other night people,

it was a relief to me to become a night person, something that was waiting for me without my realizing it, no longer did I have a need to sleep away the best time of the day-night cycle, the dark where all the most interesting things occur, love and death, meetings and obligations,

now I could adjust to this life just as I wanted to, establish my own rhythm, eat when I felt like it, go for walks without being seen except by very few, work when it pleased me, in clear and unchanging illumination, independent of the capriciousness of day, sunshine and rain, noise and disturbances, telephone signals, mail dropping into the mailbox, unexpected visits,

winter was the best time with its long, dark nights, almost too good considering that most others also became halfway night persons, one did not have exclusive rights to the night as one wanted, but still, the winter night was sufficient,

summer was trying because it forced even a night person to become halfway a day person, with all this intrusive light, people drifting around until midnight and children playing outside until far beyond bedtime, there was hardly darkness enough to venture out, only a kind of pale and false dusk, a night that was more or less lost,

I tried living with a woman, a day person, so that she would not disturb me by sharing my nights, in one way it was successful, in another way not, the advantage was that we did not see each other too often and did not wear each other out with common habits, but apparently she missed that and after some time she did not want to continue, said that it was unnatural to lead separate lives like that, and after her there was calm, if I could not always sleep all day I could merely turn the lamp on and read, make my own night in the middle of day ❧

S*uddenly, I have a problematic* relationship with the days of the week, almost a forced one that attempts to surround me like an invisible cage,

suddenly, I am gripped by a fear of Sundays that makes me unwilling to go out or to undertake anything, as if everything were doomed to failure on a Sunday,

I do not want to see anybody, cannot even make myself read a book, the day merely idles, unendingly long and still unrealistically short, since it contains nothing,

on Mondays, I rise early, full of active eagerness, everything I do is like a dance, it flows and flies away from me like the hours flow and fly away, until I finally sit there in the evening with a heap of completed work, my head dizzy as if intoxicated, but empty like an echo, a whisper,

on Tuesdays, I absolutely must go out, whatever the weather, out of the city, into forests, terrain, whether I am fried by the sun or soaking wet, I am, at any price, an outdoor person with a greed for the four elements: earth, water, air, fire,

on Wednesdays, I am caught by desire to meet friends, men and women with whom I can talk, get involved in long discussions, complicated arguments, excessive speculations and fantasies, an ultimately tiring but stimulating day,

on Thursdays, I quite naturally layer work and rest, a couple of hours of work followed by an hour of relaxation, sleep or dozing, stretched out on the sofa, it makes the day seem striped like a zebra,

on Fridays, I wake up late and feel lustful, most of all I like to spend part of the day with a woman and most of all, it is our bodies that experience each other, but there are also thoughts and conversations woven into each other,

on Saturdays, I am dreamy and thoughtful, I absentmindedly do some work, feel as if waiting for something that nevertheless does not happen, only the troublesome Sunday looms ahead,

and thus I am locked into the days of the week as in a house with seven different rooms where I move from one into the other, nobody forces me, it is all voluntary, and still, I cannot say that I want it: it must be the same feeling that a train has following its given track ♪

B*efore my hands became coarse* from farm work, I withdrew to writing and my hands became long and refined, those of a writer, at the typewriter, for I could hardly write by hand,

I have kept these hands as long as possible, true violinist hands, with narrow, elongated but fairly strong fingers that could respond to a handshake with a firm grip,

not until old age did my hands begin to change, become noticeably coarser with joints swelling, and increasingly difficult to bend, they stiffen and hide pain,

it is as if something long forgotten and overcome had returned, a coarsening and wearing out as after using heavy tools for a long time, in demanding physical work, like an inheritance that has finally caught up with me, appeared from generations long before mine,

these are hands I no longer recognize as my own, strange hands that have succeeded my own, stiffened working hands that seem to have nothing to do with lifelong writing,

I observe how little by little these hands are transformed and disfigured, turning clumsy, inflexible, hurtful until they seem increasingly inhuman, as if they were changing into some kind of deformed, grotesque claws,

they appear like the gnarled roots of trees, such as are shooting up to the soil surface and staying there, crooked and dark, with veins crawling on top of the hand, almost ready to burst through the skin over the bones, reminding me more and more of my skeleton,

and there is nothing I can do about it, I am forced to tolerate these strange hands for the rest of my days although I cannot really despise them, rather, I feel a certain compassion for them,

in this respect, all of my writ-
ing has been of no use, I could just as well have cleared fields,
dug ditches, or some other hard labor

H*ow badly suited you are for* being a hotel guest, from the very beginning you feel suspect, you use the wrong expressions even in your own language, not to mention others,

your voice is uncertain, does not quite carry, lacks the natural self-assurance that can be noticed in almost everybody else, people who seem born to be hotel guests, like fish in the water, just the right tone of superiority and confidentiality,

and when you have finally passed the purgatory of the reception desk and been assigned your room, received the key, the baggage taken care of, the room is not what you expected but something else,

a coarse substitute with hell-red or sickly greenish yellow colors, with windows looking out in the wrong direction that cannot be opened or properly closed, with the wrong kind of curtains, thick as blankets, dusty, impossible to pull aside or to close, the radiator is icily cold when it is cold outside or glowing when it is hot, and it cannot be adjusted, the bed has an intolerable feather coverlet or a worn and thin blanket at odds with the seasons, the faucets are dripping in the bathroom, the toilet flushes itself, and someone else's hair is floating everywhere,

still, the room is possible to tolerate and get used to, almost attached to, in heavy sleep and waking up late, unwilling to rise and go out into a strange city,

until the maids threaten to break into the room and throw you out, with your coat still on your arm you stumble down the stairs among bedlinen ripped out, dirty sheets and towels, the mixed smells of urine, sperm, and sweat,

and there you are standing in the lobby, half dressed and comical, hesitating about where to leave your key, whether or not to say good morning, you feel ironical looks following you, apparently wondering when you will leave, how long you can afford to stay, and what you might be doing in this city,

and when you return, it is a question of sneaking in without being noticed, if possible, preferably behind somebody else, of maneuvering to get the key and disappear up the stairs, of not waiting for the busy elevator but hurrying into your room, your haven, your burrow, where the hunters have not yet penetrated ⟨ℐ⟩

S*uddenly the bells start chiming* in the church tower on the hill and a flock of doves flies away and spreads into loosely formed bouquets circling in the space above,

at that moment one sees black rings form around the church tower and expand, spreading over the surroundings while at the same time losing their density and blackness like smoke slowly dispersing,

it is as if the dark rings followed the waves of sound from the church bells and were carried away by them, higher and higher, farther and farther away, until an enormous black-ringed dome envelops the entire neighborhood,

the doves as well, most of them white, strangely soak up the black color while circling and soon they have all turned black, sooty,

and then they start falling from space, one after the other, as if mortally wounded, fluttering sideways and tumbling through the air, then reaching the ground, lying there like bundles of black feathers

H*e turns on the screen which*
flutters at first and shows abstract patterns, while contentedly
he sinks into the armchair, stretches his legs, unbuttons his
pants at the waist and makes himself comfortable, lights a
cigarette and sees the first moving pictures through a veil of
blue smoke, the black eye which gazes out on the world has
been filled with light and he feels how the good food fills his
belly,

what he sees first are, as usual,
the wretched starving creatures who seem to wear their
skeletons outside their bodies although their stomachs are
distended like drums, hollow and emaciated faces not quite
knowing whether to smile or show their suffering, children
lie naked on the ground with comically large heads, boys'
genitals looking like curled-up snails and girl children showing a naked slit like a tightly closed mouth,

he yawns, nothing new, just
the same old world, but now there is a war, that immediately
enlivens the picture although it is far away, too far away, and
seen from a great distance, such cowards who do not dare
take any personal risks, who are positioned safely behind
telephoto lenses or maybe flying above in a helicopter,

look at these small figures, like
tin soldiers, not real, and in black and white, the blood dark
as lava and the greenery grey, explosions disappearing in
smoke and dust, houses slowly caving in or splattering all
over and in all directions, just a lot of noise and clamor, hardly a perceptible scream from someone dying, and he burps,
he has eaten a bit too much, it comes up again tasting sour
and bitter,

but now there is a beauty pag-
eant, really nice legs and protruding boobs, although all of
them look alike in their bathing suits, one can hardly follow
the curves of breasts and butts,

the cigarette is finished and he doesn't feel like another one, it burns his throat a little, but really, he feels good, has a comfortable place in this world, in the bleachers, unmoved while a little snooze creeps up on him ☊

It is the murmuring of the wind, you can see it but not hear it inside the window, you can see how the wind comes and goes in waves and makes the trees move, but the trees surely do not hear the wind, nor do they feel it clutch their branches and make them sway with a movement whose origin they may not know,

the trees know nothing about the wind that makes them move so strongly and overwhelmingly, and the wind naturally knows nothing about itself nor about the trees, what happens, happens outside themselves, however strongly they are touched by it or are a part of it,

and you are a witness to this event but have nothing to do with it, you cannot affect it, nor change it, you can only watch it passively and it would exist in the same way without your presence or your observing it,

there are so many things happening around you, independently of you, without your having anything to do with them, but still they are not without importance to you, your part of them is only an image within yourself and means nothing to what happens, making you both less significant and more free ❦

P*oor humans who drag themselves* along, imprisoned in their life patterns, poor human beings carrying their own weights like sacks of potatoes or coal, their blood which must flow both up and down their veins, the eternal passage under the sun,

poor human beings with their youthful fish-like speed of movement, happy not knowing what awaits them, the eternally elusive carrot of expectations,

the small speck of light from a poppy reflected under the chin, the face half-shadowed, the cooled fat of the breasts pulled down by their own weight, the dead meat of thighs like poles of newly peeled aspen-wood, the draped bowls of hips where the sack full of intestines rests, brutally hot and trembling,

steps, steps, who guides their steps . . . a necessity which disguises itself and becomes a temptation, a compulsion believing itself to be desire, steps which lead directly to the fire-damaged wall or straight toward the steep precipice, steps which tread where others have trod, footsteps in footsteps, compelling like railroad tracks,

the white or black cloud keeps even pace high above the head, above wheat fields, fields of clover, trampled mud, newly fallen snow: the days of life are shuffled like cards in a stack, every day in an unforeseen place, with a face of surprise,

steps, steps, no matter where you go, you still reach the same destination but you must never know it, that would ruin the entire journey,

poor humans who are lifted by a wind in an involuntary dance or are drenched by rain, heavy from wetness, like no shadows are,

poor humans rising into the air in long, light-colored swirls or sinking into the earth, into the darkness of the earth, as if into the womb of death

115

Y*ou have tried to enter the elements* but found it impossible, your human form is a stranger to them all, alien to fire and air, to earth and water,

yet you have a distant kinship with them, expelled but with an element of preserved likeness, maybe you are just too sensitive, too alienated, too cold or too hot, flesh which is not sufficiently metallic, blood which recoils at the sight of the sea, water which suffocates you, air which lets you fall,

like a stranger you are a refugee wherever in the world you travel, your ever more rapid flight makes more and more returns possible, like the shuttle in a weave growing faster and faster, demanding more and more, you must relinquish neither face nor gender, even though both tempt you, to assume the shape of a fruit, of snake or fish as possible forms with bellies gliding across the ground, through water, no matter how much you could resemble a lamp, your spirit is still something different from a flame which is lit and then blown out,

your desire may light up your dreams to become a landscape of paradise, painted by the sun with colors that are still wet, where all you need is provided for you as fruits with ennobled flesh and sweetened blood,

you can ride the lion and the tiger, still innocent animals whose eyes are not lit up with the madness of hunger, the clouds can descend like white shapes of marble onto the earth, there to graze like peaceful cattle,

but you are your own contradiction and enemy, you want to recreate everything as something else, and you search for this other in your innermost darkness, you want to pull it out from its depth, still not created and still without form, filled with a yearning which never finds its mark,

you remain your own mystery, fleeing from yourself like a swan flying off in a mirrored corridor ༺

Love *which denies itself is most* durable, maintains its never satisfied hunger, its excitement in the midst of barrenness, the most taxing days leave a blush which lasts until nightfall and seeks cover in the darkness,

such is love for this barren land which abstains from all seduction, an unreasonable love which never declared itself, love for the very earth under one's feet, for the invincible grass, for the courageous multitude of leaves, for the driving rain and the soaked clothes,

it is a love, not for moss and plumage, not for foolish flowers and tender roses which cannot even bleed, only blacken, a love for this country which is only an insignificant part of the world, half-forgotten and haunted by old ghosts of war, of the intolerable memories of cold and hunger,

it is a country, poor in the midst of its sudden treacherous wealth, suspicious of itself, with a lost pain burning below the pleasure, with a taste of bark in its mouth and the cold from rivers where the current is strong,

a country which is a stranger unto itself, with this language spoken in the villages and in the bible, with the old and the new gods who have penetrated each other while slowly being destroyed,

thunder no longer speaks, the storm is losing battles in the forests, the world is expanding and losing directions and ends, infinity and eternity are entwined, a labyrinth of opposite winds,

the longing forward and the longing backward negate one another, the iron hinges of the gates rust in the gateposts of stone, the grazing cattle wear down the hills and are helped by the rains, everything happens very slowly, and everything anxiously awaits the consequences

The daring children have fleeced the wolf and let him run away like a naked and squealing pig, they sleep with clenched fists and when they dream they grind their teeth, they have no names, not even numbers tattooed on their arms,

        they sculpt in dynamite as with toy clay and send up pigeons which explode in the air,

        knives are as natural to them as the sting to the bee, and their whistling makes the air split apart like brittle silk,

        their innocence is like a baby stroller covered with armor-plate, their never-ending play leaves only wreckage and shards,

        the beauty of the glass panes appears when they are broken, and stolen bridal gowns are to be sent aloft so that they may be raped by the wind,

        they do not wait patiently for their inheritance but throw themselves at it like a pack of robbers,

        to them there is no world, no earth, and even less a heaven, their anarchy may last for a season or for a century

A *final rain drop will cause* wonder in the hand of a child, a gable window which is never illuminated stares dejectedly out over a concrete yard and its glances rebound from the clouds of marble at the horizon,

the moon hangs over the broom crowns of the trees, shining weakly like a lamp filled with oil pressed from turnips, the deranged woman wanders aimlessly repeating names of flowers to herself, and not even a well-aimed stone can silence her,

the old iron fences with gilded tops scorn the wheat fields of memory, the big rocks lie loosely in their hollows doubting themselves, at the shores the swell washes bundles of clothes which no one bothers to gather,

it is like living in the caved-in belly of a goddess where the winds are turning in their condemnation, words crackle like snail shells under one's feet, if one sucks the pebbles of the beach they have a taste more bitter than lemon pits, bleakly grey vegetation crawls like intestines, no wind can disperse the trees of smoke,

who does not turn his back to the sun to find solace in his own shadow... the sea, like an insomniac with its eyelids white from salt, tosses in its stony bed, a green sun like a rotten lemon does not surprise anymore, green has long been an illness, while a dry state of health sounds like a racking cough in July, and many tongues try to lick a lost little breeze

Y*ou thought you understood that*
the deeper one penetrates the secrets of the universe, the
more mysterious and inexplicable they become, what human
thought had perceived as valid laws of nature rebelled against
the preconceived pattern and departed from themselves,
what one thought one knew, one constantly had to revise and
push into the realm of the unknown,

the universe at large did not seem
to know where it was going or what was happening to it,
opposing forces faced each other, matter and anti-matter,
annihilation against creation, lasting against ceasing, expan-
sion against contraction, time against space, an ongoing drama
without beginning and without end even though uncertain,

small was part of large, the disap-
pearing microcosm in the enormous universe, maybe small
and large was just a question of degrees, illusionary in themselves, maybe the whole universe contained the smallest micro-
particles, and the entire universe was perhaps only a minute
part of another universe, incomparably vaster,

nor did the smallest phenomena
obey universal laws or universal will, each and every one
wanted something for itself, turned away, rebelled, changed
in an unforeseen manner,

there seemed to be a kind of free-
dom within all lawfulness, no god ruled the events and occur-
rences, no universal Will or Intention, instead all seemed
without intention, self-generating and self-realizing in an
uninterrupted battle of changes,

man was given a reason to doubt
everything, his own surroundings and his own consciousness,
his comprehension thrown into total freedom encompassing
all and simultaneously appearing as total constraint,

no purpose, merely a contradic-
tory game of powers and tensions, seemingly solid bodies
nothing but organizations of radiation phenomena and

chemical concoctions which would in turn be dissolved or endlessly transformed, man was alone with his vertigo in the bottomless inward and outward without ends, not a grain of dust to hold on to, everything treacherously yielding in a dance of playful changes ♙

*C*onsciousness stalks in its own jungles and avoids the bloodthirsty predator, the white and black phantoms of fear, the man with his head under his arm, the woman with her back hollowed out like a tree trunk, all the dangers and traps of tribal myth,

time staggers insecurely from the crest of the present, throws its shadow onto the emptiness of the future or looks back towards green meadows, grazing cows, quiet flocks of sheep, charging horses,

it is important to choose what one wants to remember and what one wants to forget, but one threatens to merge with the other, dust filters down as through a mill and may be explosive like flour dust, or settles in layers, finally, in drifts like old, forgotten snow, no longer white but grey like crumbled wood or finely ground stone,

feet leave traces, as if someone had just stepped out of the bath or hands leave dark imprints like those of leaves in the dust

T*here are so many who always* speak about reality, but their reality is only like a grain of sand underfoot, a mist which blinds them, a chair one brings along for support when getting up,

it is reality like a pinch of salt in the armpit, it is not the wheel but the stick which is broken by the wheel, it is not the snow but the lonely snowball they squeeze in their hands until it melts and turns into water running away, the cold remaining in the hand for a while,

it is not the prison built of stone but the rusty shackle which is no longer fastened to anything, not the wall but the shadow it throws or a beam of light which is mistaken for a hole in the wall, one stumbles not on the windy crest but in the plow-furrow, not the sea but the water which splashes around in the bucket and continues to splash in the ladle,

you slip not from the tree but on the pine needles on the ground, not the animal but the fur it has lost, not the moon in space but the copper coin in the palm of your hand, it is not the foot but the shoe, always the shoe without the foot:

yes, they always speak of reality, but their reality is always very small and fleeting

For *millions of years the earth has* prepared its feast, for millions of years the earth has been calving its glaciers and brewing its steaming marshes, it has expanded its forests and nourished its oceans, prepared a feast for beings who rose from water and mud, generated warm blood in the veins and hatched thoughts in the increasingly spacious archways of the brain,

but the recognition has grown that man has failed man, he has not been able to carry his self-imposed burden without faltering and floundering, an ever more inconsiderate plunderer of the earth given to him, with recklessness and lack of vision, torn between surfeit and old hunger,

he finishes off the earthly feast and dreams vainly of other worlds, of the unreachable fruits tempting him among the suns in starry space, while lost plains have turned into deserts, the oceans have been poisoned and are now full of death, the ground has been penetrated and blasted and robbed of its treasures,

now the human lice crawl over each other, more ravenous than any other predator or insect, multiplying in blind rage, extinguishing themselves in great numbers and masses, armed beyond comprehension to rob one another,

man has abandoned man, made himself into the all-ravaging monster, closing his eyes to horror, feeling pleasure in the midst of fear, never growing to reach a common maturity, but like a coral reef dying in the sea it devours,

what return is possible, what end to this shrieking power which does not recognize its impotence . . . a violence annihilating itself ◠

But is it man who mourns earth or earth that mourns man, and how would either of them survive if, by chance, their destinies were to be separated,

it does not help to spit blood on a wall and with this blood try to draw the likeness of a sunset, it does not help to plant a thistle in one's ear or allow a mouse to live in one's anus,

the genie has escaped from the bottle and it is no longer possible to catch it or entice it back in, instead the empty bottle is filled with ants which devour a cry of distress written aslant,

the rocks are already so soft that ships run into them and rest there as in dough, the ball-shaped clocks show a global time which is nowhere fully real, and women who turn themselves into balls are just as inaccessible as if they had remained boards,

a plus is nothing but two minuses which have joined to form a cross, the confined lunatic gathers so much wisdom that the walls finally crumble, but the lunatic has become too wise to leave,

the woman who walks around with a plate of copper close to her stomach may only harbor an unrequited love for military music, while flagpole sitting has declined miserably ✂

S*tranger within me, stranger at* my side, we walk together like the body and its shadow, we sit down in the square among vagrants and visitors from farms or foreign countries, we listen to the man with the pompadour and fluttering blue lips, follow with our eyes the girl with the turkey head,

a harp of sunbeams rises above the narrow lane, and high above it the jet plane cuts like an almost transparent, silvery dragonfly through the distended blue flag of space, the bells chime, roots in the ground as if belonging to a big tree of copper,

the locked-up well keeps the secrets of its hidden water, laughter rises in a cascade like the water jet from a fountain, the knives are like fish hiding in pockets, waiting there to bound out of darkness, the dark green leather of the leaves is sweating and shines like the flanks of horses,

beyond the noise and murmurs I hear the silence of alienation like the darkness hiding on the river bottom, I live in several eras flowing in different directions like traffic on streets crossing each other: how easy to lift the past to the surface and perceive its strange reality as present, but like reflections it escapes from the hand cupped around the water,

presence is not only presence, it is also absence and distance, unknown possibilities: the present falls endlessly backwards and rises again in front of us, is born and dies in the same moment to gather at the river which flows slowly at the same time beyond us and before us,

everything travels and changes, all is strangeness, and uncertainty is the only certainty

You have seen much and yet it seems that you have forgotten even more, memory is charitable, does not pursue you with feverish images, turning walls into living tapestry,

you only have to bring forth one handful at a time, images like running water, drowning days, nights that have devoured themselves, limbs that have crumbled, fish scales growing from your shoulders, and cries from the sea, their origin never to be traced,

you are forced to be a good loser, everything has run past you and away from you, rivulets that have hardly left any traces in the sand, you didn't know that it would be too late so soon, too late to undertake this journey that cannot be completed or has no return, too late for this body writhing, intangible like smoke,

too late to go fishing and catching nothing but torn-off and already rotten fish heads, or an eel blindly escaping from the eye sockets of someone drowned, too late to sit on the rower's bench or at the tiller under the sail,

too late for this wide-brimmed, light-colored hat that has shaded a small milky way of freckles, for the briers where the rose-hips have shrunk and blackened until they scare the birds like the nipples of old women,

never again will I walk by with a pair of oars on my shoulders, never again fall into rapt contemplation of the name "Evinrude" on an outboard motor, memory is charitable with its dark drapery, a balm to the eyes with its miniature pocket mirrors that one could put into the openings of piggy-banks,

now the bed is a vehicle and a boat and a glider, floating over grass and water and tree tops without differentiation, the streets below are gutters for humanity; inexhaustible trading, foolish pride in craftsmanship, flower-girls carrying filled baskets, and impressionists, still in their red-bearded youth

*S*oon your life's day will end, *there*
is a murmur from falling rain and the wind rocks the autumn-
nal trees, your awareness of humanity is the innermost you, it
lives in the house of your body and cannot exist outside you,

it has had its time, it has to some
degree been filled with joy, more by worries and striving, by
living from one day to the next,

it has been you yourself without
your really knowing it, partly as an absence, a visitor in your
half-empty house,

now the first snow is falling, the
shroud of earth against the winter cold, and snowy down sits
like white birds on the crowns of the pine trees, swinging
back and forth and suddenly falling, dissolved into glittering
dust, like the dust that will dissolve consciousness when the
moment comes, turn into nothingness holding all it remem-
bers and all it has forgotten, experiences and insights dis-
persed and falling like snow dust,

what good has it been, why have
you been striving and worrying, looked after your house as
well as you could, has it been anything more than a piece of
driftwood carried back and forth by invisible currents, only
to come to rest in a rock crevice,

you cannot believe in a purpose
for this whole limitless universe of invisible particles in fre-
netic dance, in a meaningless pattern that is impossible to
comprehend or does not exist, only radiance and struggle,
creation and obliteration, beginning or end,

so what does your small human
consciousness mean, less than a snowflake falling from the
pine tree outside and disappearing 🦢

O*ld age, you approach impercep-*tibly from behind until your steps become one with my steps and you enter me, compress my skeleton and bend my back as if you were preparing me for walking under ever-lower ceilings, like a miller you pull your hand through my hair and leave it white,

you open the trap doors of memory so that the immediate suddenly is far away and the distant emerges, one cannot understand where life has gone so suddenly, disappeared like a rabbit around the bend of a path,

you feel both lighter and heavier, light like a pumice stone as you stride on in the wind, and heavy like a diver in his lead shoes on dry land, you can watch a naked woman without necessarily wanting to touch her, your desire is calm like a candle flame in a closed room,

youth is something moving away into the distance, but not so much behind you as ahead of you, there is something more you would like to accomplish, but it escapes you like actions in a dream,

it is as if you were wading in ever-deeper water, the current running stronger against you, although there is neither water nor current,

increasingly, your face has turned into a ravaged mask that you do not recognize, from the inside it does not feel the way it appears from the outside, what you have accomplished and what you have not seem almost to cancel each other, whatever you have owned slips out of your hands, you journey towards the end as empty-handed as in the beginning,

old age, gravestone leaning over you, its shadow ever growing